Preface

In the ever-evolving landscape of technology and software development, **Java** has maintained its prominent position as a foundational programming language, empowering developers to create robust, scalable, and platform-independent applications. As we venture into the depths of this comprehensive guide, it is essential to recognize the remarkable journey **Java** has undertaken, from its inception as a revolutionary language to its current status as an indispensable tool for modern software engineering. This book on **Core Java Programming** is not a culmination of theoretical knowledge; rather, it is a testament to the dedication, perseverance, and collective wisdom of the many professionals and educators who have contributed to its creation. It embodies the essence of years of experience, research, and practical application, designed to not only install a profound understanding of Java's core principles but also to inspire a creative and analytical approach to problem-solving in the realm of programming.

The sheer versatility of **Java**, spanning applications in diverse domains such as enterprise software, mobile development, and web applications, underscores the significance of mastering its intricacies. This book, meticulously crafted with a blend of theoretical exposition and practical examples, strives to cater to a wide spectrum of learners, including students, educators, and seasoned professionals, seeking to strengthen their foundations or enhance their expertise in this domain. Its holistic approach encompasses the essentials of Java Programming, encompassing topics ranging from Object-Oriented Programming to multithreading, exception handling, and data structures, thus providing a comprehensive framework that equips readers with the tools necessary to tackle real-world challenges.

Moreover, the pedagogical design of this book emphasizes the application of concepts through hands-on exercises, case studies, and coding challenges, fostering an immersive and engaging learning experience. By illustrating best practices, design patterns, and effective programming techniques, this guide aims to cultivate a mindset that not only focuses on writing functional code but also prioritizes efficiency, scalability, and maintainability, all crucial factors in the development of sustainable and robust software solutions.

As we delve into the intricate nuances of **Core Java Programming**, it is imperative to recognize the dynamic nature of the technological landscape, constantly evolving and demanding continuous adaptation and learning. Therefore, this book not only provides a solid foundation but also encourages readers to remain curious, open-minded, and resilient in the face of emerging paradigms and innovations. It aspires to foster a community of learners and practitioners who embrace the spirit of collaboration, innovation, and lifelong learning, ultimately contributing to the ever-expanding horizons of the Java Programming Ecosystem.

Table of Contents

1. Write a Java Program that declares and initializes variables of different data types (int, double, boolean, String)
and prints their values. Ensure that the program demonstrates the use of appropriate data types.

Code-

```
class VariableDemo {
    public static void main(String[] args) {
        // Declare and initialize variables of different data types
        int integerVariable = 40;
        double doubleVariable = 3.14;
        boolean booleanVariable = false;
        String stringVariable = "Hello, World!";

        // Print the values of the variables
        System.out.println("Integer Variable: " + integerVariable);
        System.out.println("Double Variable: " + doubleVariable);
        System.out.println("Boolean Variable: " + booleanVariable);
        System.out.println("String Variable: " + stringVariable);
    }
}
```

Output-

```
Integer Variable: 40
Double Variable: 3.14
Boolean Variable: false
String Variable: Hello, World!
```

2. Create a Java Program that converts a given double value into an integer by performing explicit type casting.
Print both the original double value and the converted integer value.

Code-

```
public class DoubleToIntConversion {
    public static void main(String[] args) {
        // Given double value
        double doubleValue = 7.76;

        // Convert the double value to an integer using explicit casting
        int intValue = (int) doubleValue;
```

```
        // Print the original double value and the converted integer value
        System.out.println("Original Double Value: " + doubleValue);
        System.out.println("Converted Integer Value: " + intValue);
    }
}
```

Output-

Original Double Value: 7.76

Converted Integer Value: 7

3. Define a constant named "PI" with a value of 3.14159 in a Java Program. Calculate and print the area of a circle with a radius of 5 using this constant.

Code-

```
public class CircleArea {
    public static final double PI = 3.14159;

    public static void main(String[] args) {
        // Given radius of the circle
        double radius = 5.0;

        // Calculate the area of the circle using the constant PI
        double area = PI * radius * radius;

        // Print the calculated area
        System.out.println("The area of the circle with a radius of " + radius + " is: " + area);
    }
}
```

Output-

The area of the circle with a radius of 5.0 is: 78.53975

4. Create a Java Program that prompts the user to enter their full name as a single String. Split the name into first name and last name, and then print both names separately.

Code-

```
import java.util.Scanner;

public class NameSplitter {
    public static void main(String[] args) {
        Scanner scanner = new Scanner(System.in);

        // Prompt the user to enter their full name
```

```
        System.out.print("Enter your full name: ");
        String fullName = scanner.nextLine();

        // Split the full name into first name and last name
        String[] nameParts = fullName.split(" ");

        // Check if there are at least two parts (first name and last name)
        if (nameParts.length >= 2) {
            String firstName = nameParts[0];
            String lastName = nameParts[nameParts.length - 1];

            // Print the first name and last name separately
            System.out.println("First Name: " + firstName);
            System.out.println("Last Name: " + lastName);
        } else {
            System.out.println("Invalid input. Please enter your full name with at least a first name
and last name.");
        }

        scanner.close();
    }
}
```

Output-

Enter your full name: Jayant Sharma
First Name: Jayant
Last Name: Sharma

5. Create a Java Program that calculates the sum of two integer variables.

Code-

```
public class IntegerVariables {
    public static void main(String[] args) {
        int num1 = 300;
        int num2 = 400;
        int sum = num1 + num2;
        System.out.println("Sum: " + sum);
    }
}
```

Output-

Sum: 700

6. Create a Java Program that calculates the product of two Floating-Point variables.

Code-

```
public class FloatingPointVariables {
   public static void main(String[] args) {
      double num1 = 3.14;
      double num2 = 1.66;
      double product = num1 * num2;
      System.out.println("Product: " + product);
   }
}
```

Output-

Product: 5.2124

7. Create a Java Program that declares and prints a character variable.

Code-

```
public class CharacterVariable {
   public static void main(String[] args) {
      char grade = 'A';
      System.out.println("Grade: " + grade);
   }
}
```

Output-

Grade: A

8. Create a Java Program that declares and prints a string variable.

Code-

```
public class StringVariable {
   public static void main(String[] args) {
      String greeting = "Hello, Java!";
      System.out.println(greeting);
   }
}
```

Output-

Hello, Java!

9. Create a Java Program that declares and prints a boolean variable.

Code-

```
public class BooleanVariable {
   public static void main(String[] args) {
      boolean isJavaFun = false;
```

```
        System.out.println("Is Java fun? " + isJavaFun);
    }
}
```

Output-

Is Java fun? false

10. Create a Java Program that converts an integer value to a double value and prints the result.

Code-

```
public class TypeConversion {
    public static void main(String[] args) {
        int intValue = 52;
        double doubleValue = (double) intValue;
        System.out.println("Double Value: " + doubleValue);
    }
}
```

Output-

Double Value: 52.0

11. Write a Java Program to demonstrate explicit narrowing conversion.

Code-

```
public class NarrowingConversion {
    public static void main(String[] args) {
        double doubleValue = 45.67;
        int intValue = (int) doubleValue;
        System.out.println("Int Value: " + intValue);
    }
}
```

Output-

Int Value: 45

12. Write a Java Program to demonstrate mixing data types.

Code-

```
public class MixingDataTypes {
    public static void main(String[] args) {
        int intValue = 50;
        char charValue = (char) intValue;
        System.out.println("Char Value: " + charValue);
    }
}
```

Output-

Char Value:2

13. Write a Java Program to demonstrate numeric promotion.

Code-

```
public class NumericPromotion {
   public static void main(String[] args) {
      byte byteValue = 10;
      int intValue = 20;
      short shortValue = 30;
      int result = byteValue + intValue + shortValue;
      System.out.println("Result: " + result);
   }
}
```

Output-

Result: 60

14. Write a Java program to demonstrate string to integer conversion.

Code-

```
public class StringToIntegerConversion {
   public static void main(String[] args) {
      String numString = "12345";
      int intValue = Integer.parseInt(numString);
      System.out.println("Integer Value: " + intValue);
   }
}
```

Output-

Integer Value: 12345

15. Write a Java program to demonstrate character to integer conversion.

Code-

```
public class CharToIntegerConversion {
   public static void main(String[] args) {
      char charValue = '9';
      int intValue = Character.getNumericValue(charValue);
      System.out.println("Integer Value: " + intValue);
   }
}
```

Output-

Integer Value: 9

Practise Questions

1. Write a Java Program that declares and initializes variables of different data types (int, double, char, boolean), and then print their values to the console.
2. Create a Java Program that demonstrates type conversion (casting) between different data types, including implicit and explicit conversions. Print the results of these conversions.
3. Write a Java Program that takes two integers as input from the user and performs arithmetic operations (addition, subtraction, multiplication, division) on them. Display the results with appropriate data type handling.
4. Develop a Java Program that prompts the user to enter a sentence as a string. Then, count and display the number of characters, words, and vowels in the sentence.
5. Write a program to print the area of a rectangle of sides 2 and 3 units respectively.
6. Write a program to print the product of the numbers 8.2 and 6.
7. Write a program to assign a value of 100.235 to a double variable and then convert it to int.
8. Write a program to add an integer variable having value 5 and a double variable having value 6.2.

1.Write a Java Program that takes two integers as input and calculates their sum, difference, product, quotient, and remainder using arithmetic operators. Display the results.

Code-

```
import java.util.Scanner;

public class ArithmeticOperations {
    public static void main(String[] args) {
        Scanner scanner = new Scanner(System.in);

        System.out.print("Enter the first integer: ");
        int num1 = scanner.nextInt();

        System.out.print("Enter the second integer: ");
        int num2 = scanner.nextInt();

        scanner.close();

        int sum = num1 + num2;
        int difference = num1 - num2;
        int product = num1 * num2;

        if (num2 != 0) {
            int quotient = num1 / num2;
            int remainder = num1 % num2;

            System.out.println("Sum: " + sum);
            System.out.println("Difference: " + difference);
            System.out.println("Product: " + product);
            System.out.println("Quotient: " + quotient);
            System.out.println("Remainder: " + remainder);
        } else {
            System.out.println("Division by zero is not allowed.");
        }
    }
}
```

Output-

```
Enter the first integer: 16
```

Enter the second integer: 5
Sum: 21
Difference: 11
Product: 80
Quotient: 3
Remainder: 1

2. **Create a Java Program that compares two numbers entered by the user and determines whether the first number is greater than, less than, equal to, or not equal to the second number. Display the comparison result.**

Code-

```
import java.util.Scanner;

public class NumberComparison {
  public static void main(String[] args) {
    Scanner scanner = new Scanner(System.in);

    System.out.print("Enter the first number: ");
    double num1 = scanner.nextDouble();

    System.out.print("Enter the second number: ");
    double num2 = scanner.nextDouble();

    scanner.close();

    if (num1 > num2) {
      System.out.println(num1 + " is greater than " + num2);
    } else if (num1 < num2) {
      System.out.println(num1 + " is less than " + num2);
    } else {
      System.out.println(num1 + " is equal to " + num2);
    }
  }
}
```

Output-

Enter the first number: 8.5
Enter the second number: 10.2
8.5 is less than 10.2

3. Write a Java Program that takes user input for two boolean values (true or false) and uses logical operators to perform AND, OR, and NOT operations on them. Display the results of each operation.

Code-

```
import java.util.Scanner;

public class LogicalOperations {
  public static void main(String[] args) {
    Scanner scanner = new Scanner(System.in);

    System.out.print("Enter the first boolean value (true or false): ");
    boolean bool1 = scanner.nextBoolean();

    System.out.print("Enter the second boolean value (true or false): ");
    boolean bool2 = scanner.nextBoolean();

    scanner.close();

    boolean andResult = bool1 && bool2;
    boolean orResult = bool1 || bool2;
    boolean notResult1 = !bool1;
    boolean notResult2 = !bool2;

    System.out.println("AND Result: " + andResult);
    System.out.println("OR Result: " + orResult);
    System.out.println("NOT Result for First Value: " + notResult1);
    System.out.println("NOT Result for Second Value: " + notResult2);
  }
}
```

Output -

```
Enter the first boolean value (true or false): true
Enter the second boolean value (true or false): false
AND Result: false
OR Result: true
NOT Result for First Value: false
NOT Result for Second Value: true
```

4. Develop a Java Program that prompts the user to enter two numbers and uses the ternary operator to find and display the larger of the two numbers.

Code-

```
import java.util.Scanner;

public class TernaryOperatorExample {
   public static void main(String[] args) {
      Scanner scanner = new Scanner(System.in);

      System.out.print("Enter the first number: ");
      double num1 = scanner.nextDouble();

      System.out.print("Enter the second number: ");
      double num2 = scanner.nextDouble();

      scanner.close();

      double largerNumber = (num1 > num2) ? num1 : num2;

      System.out.println("The larger number is: " + largerNumber);
   }
}
```

Output-

Enter the first number: 15.7
Enter the second number: 10.2
The larger number is: 15.7

5. **Create a Java Program that takes two integers as input and performs bitwise AND, OR, and XOR operations on them. Display the results in both decimal and binary formats.**

Code-

```
import java.util.Scanner;

public class BitwiseOperations {
   public static void main(String[] args) {
      Scanner scanner = new Scanner(System.in);

      System.out.print("Enter the first integer: ");
      int num1 = scanner.nextInt();

      System.out.print("Enter the second integer: ");
      int num2 = scanner.nextInt();

      scanner.close();
```

```
        // Bitwise AND
        int bitwiseAndResult = num1 & num2;
        // Bitwise OR
        int bitwiseOrResult = num1 | num2;
        // Bitwise XOR
        int bitwiseXorResult = num1 ^ num2;

        // Display results in decimal format
        System.out.println("Bitwise AND Result (Decimal): " + bitwiseAndResult);
        System.out.println("Bitwise OR Result (Decimal): " + bitwiseOrResult);
        System.out.println("Bitwise XOR Result (Decimal): " + bitwiseXorResult);

        // Display results in binary format
        System.out.println("Bitwise AND Result (Binary): " +
Integer.toBinaryString(bitwiseAndResult));
        System.out.println("Bitwise OR Result (Binary): " +
Integer.toBinaryString(bitwiseOrResult));
        System.out.println("Bitwise XOR Result (Binary): " +
Integer.toBinaryString(bitwiseXorResult));
    }
}
```

Output -

Enter the first integer: 5
Enter the second integer: 3
Bitwise AND Result (Decimal): 1
Bitwise OR Result (Decimal): 7
Bitwise XOR Result (Decimal): 6
Bitwise AND Result (Binary): 1
Bitwise OR Result (Binary): 111
Bitwise XOR Result (Binary): 110

6. **Write a Java Program to calculate the simple interest for a loan. Ask the user for the principal amount, interest rate (as a decimal), and the number of years. Calculate and display the total interest.**

Code-

```
import java.util.Scanner;

public class SimpleInterestCalculator {
```

```
    public static void main(String[] args) {
        Scanner scanner = new Scanner(System.in);
        System.out.print("Enter principal amount: ");
        double principal = scanner.nextDouble();
        System.out.print("Enter interest rate (as a decimal): ");
        double rate = scanner.nextDouble();
        System.out.print("Enter number of years: ");
        int time = scanner.nextInt();

        double simpleInterest = (principal * rate * time);
    System.out.println("Simple Interest: " + simpleInterest);
    }
}
```

Output-

Enter principal amount: 1000
Enter interest rate (as a decimal): 0.05
Enter number of years: 3
Simple Interest: 150.0

7. Develop a Java Program that converts a temperature in Fahrenheit to Celsius.

Code-

```
import java.util.Scanner;

public class FahrenheitToCelsiusConverter {
    public static void main(String[] args) {
        Scanner scanner = new Scanner(System.in);
        System.out.print("Enter temperature in Fahrenheit: ");
        double fahrenheit = scanner.nextDouble();

        double celsius = (fahrenheit - 32) * 5/9;
        System.out.println("Temperature in Celsius: " + celsius);
    }
}
```

Output-

Enter temperature in Fahrenheit: 98.6
Temperature in Celsius: 37.0

8. Create a Java Program that calculates the area of a triangle. Ask the user for the base and height of the triangle, and then compute and display the area.

Code -

```
import java.util.Scanner;

public class TriangleAreaCalculator {
    public static void main(String[] args) {
        Scanner scanner = new Scanner(System.in);
        System.out.print("Enter the base of the triangle: ");
        double base = scanner.nextDouble();
        System.out.print("Enter the height of the triangle: ");
        double height = scanner.nextDouble();

        double area = (base * height) / 2;
        System.out.println("Area of the triangle: " + area);
    }
}
```

Output-

```
Enter the base of the triangle: 5
Enter the height of the triangle: 8
Area of the triangle: 20.0
```

9. **Create a Java Program to calculate the Body Mass Index (BMI) of a person. Prompt the user to enter their weight in kilograms and height in meters, and then calculate and display the BMI.**

Code-

```
import java.util.Scanner;

public class BMICalculator {
    public static void main(String[] args) {
        Scanner scanner = new Scanner(System.in);
        System.out.print("Enter your weight in kilograms: ");
        double weight = scanner.nextDouble();
        System.out.print("Enter your height in meters: ");
        double height = scanner.nextDouble();

        double bmi = weight / (height * height);
        System.out.println("Your BMI is: " + bmi);
    }
}
```

Output-

```
Enter your weight in kilograms: 70
Enter your height in meters: 1.75
Your BMI is: 22.86
```

10. Develop a Java Program that generates and displays five random numbers between 1 and 100.

Note- Use the **java.util.Random** class to achieve this.

Code-

```
import java.util.Random;

public class RandomNumberGenerator {
  public static void main(String[] args) {
    Random random = new Random();
    System.out.println("Five random numbers between 1 and 100:");
    for (int i = 0; i < 5; i++) {
     int randomNumber = random.nextInt(100) + 1;
      System.out.println(randomNumber);
    }
  }
}
```

Output-

```
Five random numbers between 1 and 100:
72
18
91
4
35
```

11. Create a Java Program that converts a given number of days into years, months, and remaining days. Ask the user for the number of days and calculate and display the equivalent years, months, and days.

Code-

```
import java.util.Scanner;

public class DaysConverter {
  public static void main(String[] args) {
    Scanner scanner = new Scanner(System.in);
    System.out.print("Enter the number of days: ");
    int days = scanner.nextInt();
```

```
        int years = days / 365;
        int remainingDays = days % 365;
        int months = remainingDays / 30;
        int remainingDaysInMonth = remainingDays % 30;

        System.out.println(days + " days is approximately " + years + " years, " + months + " months, and " + remainingDaysInMonth + " days.");
    }
}
```

Output-

Enter the number of days: 1000
1000 days

Practise Questions

1. Write a Java Program that takes two integers as input and performs bitwise AND, OR, XOR, and left shift operations on them. Display the results of each operation.
2. Create a Java Program that evaluates a mathematical expression entered by the user. Ensure that the program correctly follows operator precedence rules.
3. Develop a Java Program that calculates the absolute value of a number entered by the user using the conditional (ternary) operator. Display the result.
4. Write a Java Program that asks the user to enter an integer and then increment it by 1 using both the pre-increment and post-increment operators. Display the results.
5. Create a Java Program that prompts the user for their age and whether they have a driver's license (true/false). Use logical operators to determine if the user is eligible to drive.
6. Develop a Java Program that calculates the remainder when one integer is divided by another. Ask the user to enter two integers and then display the remainder.
7. Write a Java Program that takes the user's first name and last name as input and concatenates them to form a full name. Display the full name as a single string.
8. Create a Java Program that compares two integers entered by the user and checks if they are equal, not equal, greater than, or less than each other. Display the comparison results.
9. Develop a Java Program that uses different assignment operators (+=, -=, *=, /=) to modify a variable's value. Ask the user for an initial value and then apply each assignment operator sequentially.
10. Write a Java Program that calculates the result of a complex arithmetic expression entered by the user. The expression should include addition, subtraction, multiplication, division, and parentheses.

1. **Write a Java Program that takes an integer input from the user and check if it is even or odd. Display an appropriate message based on the result.**

Code-

```
import java.util.Scanner;

public class EvenOddChecker {
  public static void main(String[] args) {
    Scanner scanner = new Scanner(System.in);

    System.out.print("Enter an integer: ");
    int number = scanner.nextInt();

    scanner.close();

    if (number % 2 == 0) {
      System.out.println(number + " is an even number.");
    } else {
      System.out.println(number + " is an odd number.");
    }
  }
}
```

Output -

Enter an integer: 7
7 is an odd number.

2. **Create a Java Program that prints the first 10 Fibonacci numbers using a loop (either for or while). Display the sequence.**

Code-

```
public class FibonacciSeries {
  public static void main(String[] args) {
    int n = 10; // Number of Fibonacci numbers to print
    long first = 0, second = 1;

    System.out.println("First " + n + " Fibonacci numbers:");

    for (int i = 1; i <= n; i++) {
      System.out.print(first + " ");
```

```
            long next = first + second;
            first = second;
            second = next;
        }
    }
}
```

Output -

First 10 Fibonacci numbers:
0 1 1 2 3 5 8 13 21 34

3. **Develop a Java Program that takes a numeric grade (0-100) as input and converts it to a letter grade using a switch statement. Display the letter grade (A, B, C, D, or F) based on the input.**

Code-

```
import java.util.Scanner;

public class GradeConverter {
    public static void main(String[] args) {
        Scanner scanner = new Scanner(System.in);

        System.out.print("Enter the numeric grade (0-100): ");
        int numericGrade = scanner.nextInt();

        scanner.close();

        char letterGrade;

        switch (numericGrade / 10) {
            case 10:
            case 9:
                letterGrade = 'A';
                break;
            case 8:
                letterGrade = 'B';
                break;
            case 7:
                letterGrade = 'C';
                break;
            case 6:
                letterGrade = 'D';
```

```
            break;
          default:
            letterGrade = 'F';
        }

        System.out.println("Letter Grade: " + letterGrade);
    }
}
```

Output -

Enter the numeric grade (0-100): 85
Letter Grade: B

4. Write a Java Program that uses nested loops to print a pattern of stars (*) in the shape of a right-angled triangle. The user should specify the number of rows for the triangle.

Code-

```
import java.util.Scanner;

public class RightAngleTrianglePattern {
    public static void main(String[] args) {
        Scanner scanner = new Scanner(System.in);

        System.out.print("Enter the number of rows for the right-angled triangle: ");
        int numRows = scanner.nextInt();

        scanner.close();

        // Outer loop for rows
        for (int i = 1; i <= numRows; i++) {
            // Inner loop for printing stars in each row
            for (int j = 1; j <= i; j++) {
                System.out.print("* ");
            }
            // Move to the next line to start a new row
            System.out.println();
        }
    }
}
```

Output -

Enter the number of rows for the right-angled triangle: 5
*

```
* *
* * *
* * * *
* * * * *
```

5. Create a Java Program that takes three integers as input (representing the sides of a triangle) and checks if they form an equilateral, isosceles, or scalene triangle. Display an appropriate message based on the type of triangle.

Code-

```
import java.util.Scanner;

public class TriangleTypeChecker {
  public static void main(String[] args) {
    Scanner scanner = new Scanner(System.in);

    System.out.print("Enter the length of the first side: ");
    int side1 = scanner.nextInt();

System.out.print("Enter the length of the second side: ");
    int side2 = scanner.nextInt();

    System.out.print("Enter the length of the third side: ");
    int side3 = scanner.nextInt();

    scanner.close();

    if (isValidTriangle(side1, side2, side3)) {
      if (side1 == side2 && side2 == side3) {
        System.out.println("It is an equilateral triangle.");
      } else if (side1 == side2 || side2 == side3 || side1 == side3) {
        System.out.println("It is an isosceles triangle.");
      } else {
        System.out.println("It is a scalene triangle.");
      }
    } else {
      System.out.println("The given side lengths do not form a valid triangle.");
    }
  }

  // Check if the given side lengths form a valid triangle
```

```
    public static boolean isValidTriangle(int side1, int side2, int side3) {
        return (side1 + side2 > side3) && (side1 + side3 > side2) && (side2 + side3 > side1);
    }
}
```

Output-

Enter the length of the first side: 5
Enter the length of the second side: 5
Enter the length of the third side: 5
It is an equilateral triangle.

6. Create a Java Program that check if a number is positive or negative.

Code-

```
import java.util.Scanner;

public class PositiveNegative {
    public static void main(String[] args) {
        Scanner scanner = new Scanner(System.in);
        System.out.print("Enter a number: ");
        int num = scanner.nextInt();

        if (num > 0) {
            System.out.println("Positive");
        } else if (num < 0) {
            System.out.println("Negative");
        } else {
            System.out.println("Zero");
        }
        scanner.close();
    }
}
```

Output-

Enter a number: 56
Positive

7. Create a Java Program that check if a person is eligible to vote.

Code-

```
import java.util.Scanner;

public class EligibleToVote {
    public static void main(String[] args) {
```

```
        Scanner scanner = new Scanner(System.in);
        System.out.print("Enter your age: ");
        int age = scanner.nextInt();

        if (age >= 18) {
            System.out.println("You are eligible to vote.");
        } else {
            System.out.println("You are not eligible to vote.");
        }
        scanner.close();
    }
}
```

Output-

Enter your age: 34
You are eligible to vote.

8. Create a Java Program that determine the largest of three numbers.

Code-

```
import java.util.Scanner;

public class LargestNumber {
    public static void main(String[] args) {
        Scanner scanner = new Scanner(System.in);
        System.out.print("Enter three numbers separated by spaces: ");
        int num1 = scanner.nextInt();
        int num2 = scanner.nextInt();
        int num3 = scanner.nextInt();

        int largest = num1;
        if (num2 > largest) {
            largest = num2;
        }
        if (num3 > largest) {
            largest = num3;
        }

        System.out.println("The largest number is: " + largest);
        scanner.close();
    }
}
```

Output-

Enter three numbers separated by spaces: 3 16 57
The largest number is: 57

9. Create a Java Program that determine if a year is a leap year.

Code-

```
import java.util.Scanner;

public class LeapYear {
    public static void main(String[] args) {
        Scanner scanner = new Scanner(System.in);
        System.out.print("Enter a year: ");
        int year = scanner.nextInt();

        if ((year % 4 == 0 && year % 100 != 0) || (year % 400 == 0)) {
            System.out.println(year + " is a leap year.");
        } else {
            System.out.println(year + " is not a leap year.");
        }
        scanner.close();
    }
}
```

Output-

Enter a year: 2000
2000 is a leap year.

10. Create a Java Program that check if a character is a vowel or consonant.

Code-

```
import java.util.Scanner;

public class VowelConsonant {
    public static void main(String[] args) {
        Scanner scanner = new Scanner(System.in);
        System.out.print("Enter a character: ");
        char ch = scanner.next().charAt(0);

        if (ch == 'a' || ch == 'e' || ch == 'i' || ch == 'o' || ch == 'u' ||
            ch == 'A' || ch == 'E' || ch == 'I' || ch == 'O' || ch == 'U') {
            System.out.println(ch + " is a vowel.");
        } else {
```

```
            System.out.println(ch + " is a consonant.");
        }
        scanner.close();
    }
}
```

Output-

Enter a character: M

M is a consonant.

11. Create a Java Program that check if a year is a century year.

Code-

```
import java.util.Scanner;

public class CenturyYear {
    public static void main(String[] args) {
        Scanner scanner = new Scanner(System.in);
        System.out.print("Enter a year: ");
        int year = scanner.nextInt();

        if (year % 100 == 0) {
            System.out.println(year + " is a century year.");
        } else {
            System.out.println(year + " is not a century year.");
        }
        scanner.close();
    }
}
```

Output-

Enter a year: 2001

2001 is not a century year.

12. Create a Java Program to create a simple calculator using switch case.

Code-

```
import java.util.Scanner;

public class Calculator {
    public static void main(String[] args) {
        Scanner scanner = new Scanner(System.in);
        System.out.print("Enter operator (+, -, *, /): ");
        char operator = scanner.next().charAt(0);
```

```
        System.out.print("Enter two numbers: ");
        double num1 = scanner.nextDouble();
        double num2 = scanner.nextDouble();

        double result;
        switch (operator) {
            case '+':
                result = num1 + num2;
                break;
            case '-':
                result = num1 - num2;
                break;
            case '*':
                result = num1 * num2;
                break;
            case '/':
                result = num1 / num2;
                break;
            default:
                System.out.println("Invalid operator");
                return;
        }

        System.out.println("Result: " + result);
        scanner.close();
    }
}
```

Output-

Enter operator (+, -, *, /): -
Enter two numbers: 2 5
Result: -3.0

13. Create a Java Program that determines the number of days in a given month.

Code-

```
import java.util.Scanner;

public class DaysInMonth {
    public static void main(String[] args) {
        Scanner scanner = new Scanner(System.in);
```

```
        System.out.print("Enter a month (1-12): ");
        int month = scanner.nextInt();

        int days;
        switch (month) {
            case 4:
            case 6:
            case 9:
            case 11:
                days = 30;
                break;
            case 2:
                days = 28;
                break;
default:
                days = 31;
        }

        System.out.println("Number of days: " + days);
        scanner.close();
    }
}
```

Output-

Enter a month (1-12): 11
Number of days: 30

14. Write a Java Program that calculates and displays a message based on a student's grade. The program should prompt the user to enter their grade (A, B, C, D, F), and then it should use a switch statement to provide an appropriate message for that grade. If an invalid grade is entered, it should display "Invalid grade.

Code-

```
import java.util.Scanner;

public class GradeCalculator {
    public static void main(String[] args) {
        Scanner scanner = new Scanner(System.in);
        System.out.print("Enter your grade (A, B, C, D, F): ");
        char grade = scanner.next().charAt(0);

        switch (grade) {
```

```
        case 'A':
            System.out.println("Excellent!");
            break;
        case 'B':
            System.out.println("Good job!");
            break;
    case 'C':
            System.out.println("Satisfactory.");
            break;
        case 'D':
            System.out.println("Needs improvement.");
            break;
        case 'F':
            System.out.println("You failed.");
            break;
        default:
            System.out.println("Invalid grade.");
      }
      scanner.close();
   }
}
```

Output-

Enter your grade (A, B, C, D, F): D
Needs improvement.

15. Write a Java Program that takes a month number (1-12) as input and determines the corresponding month name.

Code-

```
import java.util.Scanner;

public class MonthName {
   public static void main(String[] args) {
      Scanner scanner = new Scanner(System.in);
      System.out.print("Enter a month number (1-12): ");
      int month = scanner.nextInt();

      String monthName;
      switch (month) {
         case 1:
            monthName = "January";
```

```
            break;
        case 2:
            monthName = "February";
            break;
          // Add cases for other months
          default:
            monthName = "Invalid month";
      }

      System.out.println("Month: " + monthName);
      scanner.close();
   }
}
```

Output-

Enter a month number (1-12): 5
Month: Invalid month

16. Write a Java Program to simulate a traffic light.

Code-

```
import java.util.Scanner;

public class TrafficLight {
   public static void main(String[] args) {
      Scanner scanner = new Scanner(System.in);
      System.out.print("Enter a color (red, yellow, green): ");
      String color = scanner.nextLine().toLowerCase();

      switch (color) {
         case "red":
            System.out.println("Stop!");
            break;
         case "yellow":
            System.out.println("Slow down.");
            break;
         case "green":
            System.out.println("Go!");
            break;
         default:
            System.out.println("Invalid color");
      }
```

```
        scanner.close();
    }
}
```

Output-

Enter a color (red, yellow, green): red
Stop!

17. Create a Java Program that determines the season based on the input month (1-12).

Code-

```
import java.util.Scanner;

public class Season {
    public static void main(String[] args) {
        Scanner scanner = new Scanner(System.in);
        System.out.print("Enter a month (1-12): ");
        int month = scanner.nextInt();

        String season;
      switch (month) {
            case 12:
            case 1:
            case 2:
                season = "Winter";
                break;
            case 3:
            case 4:
            case 5:
                season = "Spring";
                break;
            case 6:
            case 7:
            case 8:
                season = "Summer";
                break;
            case 9:
            case 10:
            case 11:
                season = "Fall";
                break;
            default:
```

```
            season = "Invalid month";
        }

        System.out.println("Season: " + season);
        scanner.close();
    }
}
```

Output-

Enter a month (1-12): 5

Season: Spring

18. Write a Java Program that takes an input value representing a day of the week (1-7) and determines the corresponding day name.

Code-

```
import java.util.Scanner;

public class WeekdayName {
    public static void main(String[] args) {
        Scanner scanner = new Scanner(System.in);
        System.out.print("Enter a day of the week (1-7): ");
        int day = scanner.nextInt();

        String dayName;
        switch (day) {
            case 1:
                dayName = "Sunday";
                break;
  case 2:
                dayName = "Monday";
                break;
            // Add cases for other days
            default:
                dayName = "Invalid day";
        }

        System.out.println("Day: " + dayName);
        scanner.close();
    }
}
```

Output-

Enter a day of the week (1-7): 6
Day: Invalid day

19. Write a Java Program that takes an input number (N) and uses a while loop to count from 1 to N, displaying the numbers sequentially separated by spaces.

Code-

```
import java.util.Scanner;

public class CountingWithWhile {
  public static void main(String[] args) {
    Scanner scanner = new Scanner(System.in);
    System.out.print("Enter a number (N): ");
    int N = scanner.nextInt();

    int i = 1;
    while (i <= N) {
      System.out.print(i + " ");
      i++;
    }
    scanner.close();
  }
}
```

Output-

Enter a number (N): 45
1 2 3 4 5 6 7 8 9 10 11 12 13 14 15 16 17 18 19 20 21 22 23 24 25 26 27 28 29 30 31 32 33 34 35 36 37 38 39 40 41 42 43 44 45

20. Write a Java Program that calculates and displays the sum of all numbers from 1 to N, where N is an input number provided by the user.

Code-

```
import java.util.Scanner;

public class SumWithWhile {
  public static void main(String[] args) {
    Scanner scanner = new Scanner(System.in);
    System.out.print("Enter a number (N): ");
    int N = scanner.nextInt();

    int sum = 0;
    int i = 1;
```

```
        while (i <= N) {
          sum += i;
            i++;
        }
        System.out.println("Sum of numbers from 1 to " + N + ": " + sum);
        scanner.close();
    }
}
```

Output-

Enter a number (N): 22
Sum of numbers from 1 to 22: 253

21. Create a Java Program that takes an input number (N) and counts down from N to 1, displaying the numbers in reverse order separated by spaces.

Code-

```
import java.util.Scanner;

public class CountdownWithWhile {
    public static void main(String[] args) {
        Scanner scanner = new Scanner(System.in);
        System.out.print("Enter a number (N): ");
        int N = scanner.nextInt();

        int i = N;
        while (i >= 1) {
            System.out.print(i + " ");
            i--;
        }
      scanner.close();
    }
}
```

Output-

Enter a number (N): 6
6 5 4 3 2 1

22. Write a Java Program that calculates and displays the factorial of a given number (N).

Code-

```
import java.util.Scanner;

public class FactorialWithWhile {
```

```
    public static void main(String[] args) {
        Scanner scanner = new Scanner(System.in);
        System.out.print("Enter a number (N): ");
        int N = scanner.nextInt();

        int factorial = 1;
        int i = 1;
        while (i <= N) {
            factorial *= i;
            i++;
        }
        System.out.println(N + "! = " + factorial);
        scanner.close();
    }
}
```

Output-

```
Enter a number (N): 5
5! = 120
```

23. Create a Java Program that implements a number guessing game. The program should generate a random number between 1 and 100, and the user needs to guess that number. After each guess, the program should provide hints such as "Try higher!" or "Try lower!" until the user correctly guesses the number.

Code-

```
import java.util.Random;
import java.util.Scanner;

public class NumberGuessGame {
    public static void main(String[] args) {
        Scanner scanner = new Scanner(System.in);
        Random rand = new Random();
        int targetNumber = rand.nextInt(100) + 1; // Generate a random number between 1 and 100

        int attempts = 0;
        int guess;

        do {
            System.out.print("Guess the number (1-100): ");
            guess = scanner.nextInt();
            attempts++;
```

```
            if (guess < targetNumber) {
                System.out.println("Try higher!");
            } else if (guess > targetNumber) {
                System.out.println("Try lower!");
            }
        } while (guess != targetNumber);

        System.out.println("Congratulations! You guessed the number in " + attempts + " attempts.");
        scanner.close();
    }
}
```

Output-

Guess the number (1-100): 66

Try lower!

24. Write a Java Program that takes an input number (N) and prints all even numbers from 2 up to N (inclusive) using while loop.

Code-

```
import java.util.Scanner;

public class EvenNumbersWithWhile {
    public static void main(String[] args) {
        Scanner scanner = new Scanner(System.in);
        System.out.print("Enter a number (N): ");
        int N = scanner.nextInt();

        int i = 2;
        while (i <= N) {
            System.out.print(i + " ");
            i += 2;
        }
        scanner.close();
    }
}
```

Output-

Enter a number (N): 65

2 4 6 8 10 12 14 16 18 20 22 24 26 28 30 32 34 36 38 40 42 44 46 48 50 52 54 56 58 60 62 64

25. Create a Java Program for password validation. The program should compare the user's input password with a predefined password, which is "secret123".

Code-

```
import java.util.Scanner;

public class PasswordValidation {
  public static void main(String[] args) {
    Scanner scanner = new Scanner(System.in);
    String password = "secret123";

    int attempts = 3;
    while (attempts > 0) {
      System.out.print("Enter the password: ");
      String userPassword = scanner.next();

      if (userPassword.equals(password)) {
        System.out.println("Access granted!");
        break;
      } else {
        System.out.println("Incorrect password. " + (--attempts) + " attempts left.");
      }
    }

    if (attempts == 0) {
      System.out.println("Access denied. Too many incorrect attempts.");
    }
    scanner.close();
  }
}
```

Output-

Enter the password: 765

Incorrect password. 2 attempts left.

26. Write a Java Program that generates a multiplication table for a given number using while loop.

Code-

```
import java.util.Scanner;

public class MultiplicationTable {
  public static void main(String[] args) {
```

```
        Scanner scanner = new Scanner(System.in);
        System.out.print("Enter a number: ");
        int num = scanner.nextInt();

        int i = 1;
        while (i <= 10) {
            System.out.println(num + " x " + i + " = " + (num * i));
            i++;
        }
        scanner.close();
    }
}
```

Output-

Enter a number: 6

6 x 1 = 66 x 2 = 126 x 3 = 186 x 4 = 246 x 5 = 306 x 6 = 366 x 7 = 426 x 8 = 486 x 9 = 546 x 10 = 60

27. Create a Java Program for a menu-driven application. The program should display a menu with options to print "Hello," "World," or "Exit." Users should enter their choice (1, 2, or 3) and get the corresponding output or exit the program, if they choose "Exit." If an invalid choice is entered, then the program should display "Invalid choice. Try again." until the user selects a valid option.

Code-

```
import java.util.Scanner;

public class MenuDrivenProgram {
    public static void main(String[] args) {
        Scanner scanner = new Scanner(System.in);
        int choice;

        do {
            System.out.println("Menu:");
            System.out.println("1. Print Hello");
            System.out.println("2. Print World");
            System.out.println("3. Exit");
            System.out.print("Enter your choice: ");
            choice = scanner.nextInt();

            switch (choice) {
                case 1:
```

```
                System.out.println("Hello");
                break;
            case 2:
                System.out.println("World");
                break;
    case 3:
                System.out.println("Exiting program.");
                break;
            default:
                System.out.println("Invalid choice. Try again.");
        }
      } while (choice != 3);

      scanner.close();
   }
}
```

Output-

Menu:
1. Print Hello
2. Print World
3. Exit
Enter your choice: 2

Practise Questions

1. Write a Java Program to find the GCD of two numbers using while loop.
2. Write a Java Program to reverse a number using recursion.
3. Write a Java Program to find the sum of all even numbers between 1 and 100 using a continue statement.
4. Write a Java Program to check whether a character is a vowel or consonant using an if-else ladder.
5. Write a Java Program to find the GCD of two numbers using while loop.
6. Write a Java Program to check whether a number is Armstrong or not using for loop.
7. Write a Java Program to check whether a string is palindrome or not using do-while loop.
8. Write a Java Program to find the sum of digits of a number using recursion.
9. Write a Java Program to check whether a number is a perfect number or not using nested for loop.
10. Write a Java Program to convert decimal to binary using bitwise operator.
11. Write a Java Program to find the sum of all prime numbers between 1 and 100 using continue statement.
12. Write a Java Program to check whether a year is a leap year or not using if-else ladder.
13. Write a Java Program to check whether a number is a palindrome or not using while loop.
14. Write a Java Program to find the sum of digits of a number using do-while loop.
15. Write a Java Program to check whether a number is a perfect square or not using for loop.

1. Write a Java Program that takes the user's name as input and then prints a personalized greeting message.

Code-

```
import java.util.Scanner;

public class GreetingProgram {
    public static void main(String[] args) {
        Scanner scanner = new Scanner(System.in);

        System.out.print("Enter your name: ");
        String name = scanner.nextLine();

  System.out.println("Hello, " + name + "! Welcome to our program.");

        scanner.close();
    }
}
```

Output -

Enter your name: Jay
Hello, Jay! Welcome to our program.

2. Write a Java Program that takes a password from the user without displaying it on the console and then verifies it.

Code-

```
import java.io.Console;

public class PasswordVerifier {
    public static void main(String[] args) {
        Console console = System.console();

        if (console == null) {
            System.err.println("Console not available.");
            System.exit(1);
        }

        char[] password = console.readPassword("Enter your password: ");

        // Check if the password is "secret"
```

```
        if (new String(password).equals("secret")) {
            System.out.println("Access granted.");
        } else {
            System.out.println("Access denied.");
        }
    }
}
```

Output -

Enter your password:

(Password input is not displayed)

Access granted.

3. Create a Java Program that takes an integer as input and prints its square.

Code-

```
import java.util.Scanner;

public class SquareCalculator {
    public static void main(String[] args) {
        Scanner scanner = new Scanner(System.in);
        System.out.print("Enter an integer: ");
        int number = scanner.nextInt();
        int square = number * number;
        System.out.println("The square of " + number + " is " + square);
        scanner.close();
    }
}
```

Output –

Enter an integer: 5

The square of 5 is 25

4. Write a Java Program that reads a line of text from the user and then displays it in reverse order.

Code-

```
import java.util.Scanner;

public class ReverseString {
    public static void main(String[] args) {
        Scanner scanner = new Scanner(System.in);
        System.out.print("Enter a string: ");
        String input = scanner.nextLine();
        String reversed = new StringBuilder(input).reverse().toString();
```

```
        System.out.println("Reversed string: " + reversed);
        scanner.close();
    }
}
```

Output-

Enter a string: Hello, World!

Reversed string: !dlroW ,olleH

5. Create a Java Program that takes two floating-point numbers as input and calculates their sum and average.

Code-

```
import java.util.Scanner;

public class SumAndAverage {
    public static void main(String[] args) {
        Scanner scanner = new Scanner(System.in);
        System.out.print("Enter the first number: ");
        double num1 = scanner.nextDouble();
        System.out.print("Enter the second number: ");
double num2 = scanner.nextDouble();
        double sum = num1 + num2;
        double average = sum / 2;
        System.out.println("Sum: " + sum);
        System.out.println("Average: " + average);
        scanner.close();
    }
}
```

Output-

Enter the first number: 10.5

Enter the second number: 7.5

Sum: 18.0

Average: 9.0

6. Write a Java Program that prompts the user to enter their name and age and then displays a greeting message with their age.

Code-

```
import java.util.Scanner;

public class AgeGreeting {
    public static void main(String[] args) {
```

```
        Scanner scanner = new Scanner(System.in);
        System.out.print("Enter your name: ");
        String name = scanner.nextLine();
        System.out.print("Enter your age: ");
        int age = scanner.nextInt();
        System.out.println("Hello, " + name + "! You are " + age + " years old.");
        scanner.close();
    }
}
```

Output-

Enter your name: Alice
Enter your age: 30
Hello, Alice! You are 30 years old.

Practise Questions

1. Write a Java Program to read a text file and count the number of words in it. Assume that words are separated by spaces.
2. Create a Java Program that calculates the area and perimeter of a rectangle and displays the results with proper formatting.
3. Create a Java Program that takes the name and age of a person as input and displays a personalized message.
4. Create a Java Program that takes an integer as input and checks if it's positive, negative, or zero.
5. Write a Java Program that takes a password as input and checks if it matches a predefined password. Display access granted or denied accordingly.
6. Create a Java Program that reads a series of numbers from the user until they enter a negative number. Display the sum of the positive numbers.
7. Create a Java Program that takes a sentence as input and counts the number of uppercase and lowercase characters.

1.Write a Java Program that attempts to divide a number by zero. Handle the ArithmeticException and display a custom error message.

Code-

```
public class ArithmeticExceptionHandling {
   public static void main(String[] args) {
      try {
         int result = 10 / 0;
         System.out.println("Result: " + result);
      } catch (ArithmeticException e) {
  System.err.println("Error: Division by zero is not allowed.");
      }
   }
}
```

Output -

Error: Division by zero is not allowed.

2. Write a Java Program that attempts to access a method on a null object reference. Handle the NullPointerException and display a custom error message.

Code-

```
public class NullPointerExceptionHandling {
   public static void main(String[] args) {
      try {
         String str = null;
         int length = str.length();
         System.out.println("String Length: " + length);
      } catch (NullPointerException e) {
         System.err.println("Error: Null reference encountered.");
      }
   }
}
```

Output:

Error: Null reference encountered.

3. Write a Java Program that attempts to read from a non-existent file. Handle the FileNotFoundException and display a custom error message.

Code-

```
import java.io.*;
```

```
public class FileReadExceptionHandling {
   public static void main(String[] args) {
      try {
 BufferedReader reader = new BufferedReader(new FileReader("nonexistent.txt"));
         String line = reader.readLine();
         reader.close();
         System.out.println("Line: " + line);
      } catch (FileNotFoundException e) {
  System.err.println("Error: File not found.");
      } catch (IOException e) {
         System.err.println("Error: An I/O error occurred.");
      }
   }
}
```

Output -

Error: File not found.

4. Create a Java Program that demonstrates concept of basic Exception Handling.

Code-

```
public class ExceptionHandlingExample1 {
   public static void main(String[] args) {
      try {
         int result = 10 / 0; // ArithmeticException
      } catch (ArithmeticException e) {
         System.out.println("Arithmetic Exception: " + e.getMessage());
      }
   }
}
```

Output-

Arithmetic Exception: / by zero

5. Create a Java Program using finally block.

Code-

```
public class ExceptionHandlingExample3 {
   public static void main(String[] args) {
      try {
         int result = 10 / 0; // ArithmeticException
      } catch (ArithmeticException e) {
         System.out.println("Arithmetic Exception: " + e.getMessage());
```

```
        } finally {
            System.out.println("Finally block executed.");
        }
    }
}
```
Output-

Arithmetic Exception: / by zero
Finally block executed.

6. Write a Java Program that demonstrates the concept of handling multiple exceptions. The program should contain code that intentionally triggers both an ArrayIndexOutOfBoundsException and a generic Exception.

Code-

```
public class ExceptionHandlingExample2 {
    public static void main(String[] args) {
        try {
            int[] arr = new int[5];
            arr[10] = 5; // ArrayIndexOutOfBoundsException
        } catch (ArrayIndexOutOfBoundsException e) {
            System.out.println("Array Index Out of Bounds: " + e.getMessage());
        } catch (Exception e) {
            System.out.println("Generic Exception: " + e.getMessage());
        }
    }
}
```
Output-

Array Index Out of Bounds: Index 10 out of bounds for length 5

7. Caught Exception: Custom Exception

Code-

```
public class ExceptionHandlingExample4 {
    public static void main(String[] args) {
        try {
            throw new RuntimeException("Custom Exception");
        } catch (RuntimeException e) {
            System.out.println("Caught Exception: " + e.getMessage());
        }
    }
}
```
Output-

Caught Exception: Custom Exception

8. Write a Java Program that demonstrates the concept of rethrowing an exception with a custom error message.

Code-

```
public class ExceptionHandlingExample7 {
  public static void main(String[] args) {
    try {
      int result = 10 / 0; // ArithmeticException
    } catch (ArithmeticException e) {
      System.out.println("Arithmetic Exception: " + e.getMessage());
      throw e; // Rethrowing the exception
    }
  }
}
```

Output-

Arithmetic Exception: / by zero
Exception in thread "main" java.lang.ArithmeticException: Custom error message.

9. Create a Java Program that demonstrates the concept of Custom Exception Handling in Threads

Code-

```
public class ExceptionHandlingExample9 {
  public static void main(String[] args) {
    try {
      int result = 10 / 0; // ArithmeticException
    } catch (ArithmeticException e) {
      try {
        throw new RuntimeException("Runtime Exception", e);
      } catch (RuntimeException re) {
        System.out.println("Chained Exception: " + re.getMessage());
        System.out.println("Original Cause: " + re.getCause().getMessage());
      }
    }
  }
}
```

Output-

Chained Exception: Runtime Exception
Original Cause: / by zero

Practise Questions

1. Write a Java Program that attempts to perform different operations (e.g., division and array access) inside a loop and handles multiple types of exceptions using separate catch blocks.
2. Create a custom exception called InvalidAgeException. Write a Java Program that takes a person's age as input and throws InvalidAgeException if the age is less than 0 or greater than 150.
3. Create a Java Program with multiple methods, including a divide method that throws an ArithmeticException. Call this method from the main method and handle the exception there.
4. Write a Java Program that demonstrates chained exceptions by throwing an exception from within another exception's catch block.
5. Write a Java Program that reads data from a text file ("data.txt") using FileReader. If an IOException occurs, catch it, display a custom error message, and rethrow it as an unchecked exception.

1. Write a Java Program that defines a custom exception class and throws it when a certain condition is met.

Code-

```
class CustomException extends Exception {
    public CustomException(String message) {
        super(message);
    }
}

public class CustomExceptionHandling {
    public static void main(String[] args) {
        try {
            int age = 13;
            if (age < 18) {
                throw new CustomException("Error: You must be at least 18 years old.");
            }
            System.out.println("Access granted.");
        } catch (CustomException e) {
            System.err.println(e.getMessage());
        }
    }
}
```

Output -

Error: You must be at least 18 years old.

2. Write a Java Program that attempts to access an element in an array at an invalid index. Handle the ArrayIndexOutOfBoundsException and display a custom error message.

Code-

```
public class ArrayIndexExceptionHandling {
    public static void main(String[] args) {
        try {
            int[] arr = {1, 2, 3};
            int element = arr[5];
          System.out.println("Element: " + element);
        } catch (ArrayIndexOutOfBoundsException e) {
            System.err.println("Error: Array index out of bounds.");
        }
```

```
    }
}
```

Output-

Error: Array index out of bounds.

3. Write a Java Program that defines a custom exception class named "NegativeValueException" and throws it when a negative value is encountered while calculating the area of a rectangle.

Code-

```
class NegativeValueException extends Exception {
    public NegativeValueException(String message) {
        super(message);
    }
}

public class RectangleAreaCalculator {
    public static int calculateArea(int length, int width) throws NegativeValueException {
        if (length < 0 || width < 0) {
          throw new NegativeValueException("Error: Length and width cannot be negative.");
        }
        return length * width;
    }

    public static void main(String[] args) {
        try {
            int area = calculateArea(5, -3);
            System.out.println("Area of rectangle: " + area);
        } catch (NegativeValueException e) {
            System.err.println(e.getMessage());
        }
    }
}
```

Output-

Error: Length and width cannot be negative.

4. Create a Java Program that defines a custom exception class called "InsufficientBalanceException" and throws it when a bank account withdrawal exceeds the available balance. Provide the program and expected output.

Code-

```
class InsufficientBalanceException extends Exception {
    public InsufficientBalanceException(String message) {
        super(message);
    }
}

public class BankAccount {
    private double balance;

    public BankAccount(double initialBalance) {
        balance = initialBalance;
    }

    public void withdraw(double amount) throws InsufficientBalanceException {
        if (amount > balance) {
            throw new InsufficientBalanceException("Error: Insufficient balance to withdraw.");
        }
        balance -= amount;
    }

    public static void main(String[] args) {
        try {
            BankAccount account = new BankAccount(1000);
            account.withdraw(1500);
            System.out.println("Withdrawal successful.");
        } catch (InsufficientBalanceException e) {
            System.err.println(e.getMessage());
        }
    }
}
```

Output-

Error: Insufficient balance to withdraw.

5. Write a Java program that defines a custom exception class "FileNotFoundException" and throws it when a file with a specific name cannot be found during file operations.

Code-

```
class FileNotFoundException extends Exception {
  public FileNotFoundException(String message) {
    super(message);
  }
}

public class FileOperations {
  public static void openFile(String filename) throws FileNotFoundException {
    if (!filename.equals("sample.txt")) {
      throw new FileNotFoundException("Error: File not found.");
    }
    System.out.println("File opened successfully.");
  }

  public static void main(String[] args) {
    try {
      openFile("file.txt");
    } catch (FileNotFoundException e) {
      System.err.println(e.getMessage());
    }
  }
}
```

Output-

Error: File not found.

6. Create a Java Program that defines a custom exception class "InvalidInputException" and throws it when a user enters an invalid input, such as a non-numeric value.

Code-

```
class InvalidInputException extends Exception {
  public InvalidInputException(String message) {
super(message);
  }
}

public class UserInputValidation {
```

```
    public static int parseInteger(String input) throws InvalidInputException {
        try {
            return Integer.parseInt(input);
        } catch (NumberFormatException e) {
            throw new InvalidInputException("Error: Invalid input. Please enter a valid integer.");
        }
    }

    public static void main(String[] args) {
        try {
            int value = parseInteger("abc");
            System.out.println("Parsed value: " + value);
        } catch (InvalidInputException e) {
            System.err.println(e.getMessage());
        }
    }
}
```

Output-

Error: Invalid input. Please enter a valid integer.

7. Write a Java Program that defines a custom exception class "PermissionDeniedException" and throws it when a user attempts to access a restricted resource without proper permissions.

Code-

```
class PermissionDeniedException extends Exception {
    public PermissionDeniedException(String message) {
        super(message);
    }
}

public class ResourceAccess {
    public static void grantAccess(boolean hasPermission) throws PermissionDeniedException {
        if (!hasPermission) {
            throw new PermissionDeniedException("Error: Permission denied.");
        }
        System.out.println("Access granted.");
    }

public static void main(String[] args) {
        try {
```

```
            grantAccess(false);
        } catch (PermissionDeniedException e) {
            System.err.println(e.getMessage());
        }
    }
}
```

Output-

Error: Permission denied.

Practise Questions

1. Create a Java Program that defines a custom exception class "DivisionByZeroException" and throws it when a user attempts to divide a number by zero.
2. Write a Java Program that defines a custom exception class "InvalidInputRangeException" and throws it when a user enters a number outside a specified range (e.g., between 1 and 100).
3. Create a Java Program that defines a custom exception class "InvalidPasswordLengthException" and throws it when a user tries to set a password with fewer than 8 characters.
4. Write a Java Program that defines a custom exception class "OutOfStockException" and throws it when a user tries to purchase an item that is out of stock.
5. Create a Java Program that defines a custom exception class "InvalidDateException" and throws it when a user enters an invalid date (e.g., February 30th).
6. Write a Java Program that defines a custom exception class "UsernameTakenException" and throws it when a user tries to register with a username that is already in use.
7. Create a Java Program that defines a custom exception class "InvalidInputException" and throws it when a user enters a negative number as input for calculating the square root.

1. **Write a Java Program that demonstrates multithreading using the Runnable interface. Create two threads that print numbers from 1 to 10 simultaneously.**

Code-

```
public class MultiThreadRunnable {
    public static void main(String[] args) {
        Runnable task = () -> {
            for (int i = 1; i <= 10; i++) {
                System.out.println(Thread.currentThread().getName() + ": " + i);
            }
        };

        Thread thread1 = new Thread(task);
        Thread thread2 = new Thread(task);

        thread1.start();
        thread2.start();
    }
}
```

Output -

```
Thread-0: 1
Thread-1: 1
Thread-0: 2
Thread-1: 2
Thread-0: 3
Thread-1: 3
    ...
```

2. **Write a Java Program that demonstrates synchronization using locks. Create two threads that increment a shared counter using a Lock object to ensure proper synchronization.**

Code-

```
import java.util.concurrent.locks.Lock;
import java.util.concurrent.locks.ReentrantLock;

public class SynchronizationWithLocks {
    private static int counter = 0;
    private static Lock lock = new ReentrantLock();

    public static void main(String[] args) {
```

```
        Runnable task = () -> {
            for (int i = 0; i < 10000; i++) {
                incrementCounter();
            }
        };

        Thread thread1 = new Thread(task);
        Thread thread2 = new Thread(task);

        thread1.start();
        thread2.start();

        try {
            thread1.join();
            thread2.join();
        } catch (InterruptedException e) {
            e.printStackTrace();
        }

        System.out.println("Final Counter Value: " + counter);
    }

    private static void incrementCounter() {
        lock.lock();
        try {
            counter++;
        } finally {
            lock.unlock();
        }
    }
}
```

Output-

Final Counter Value: 20000

3. **Write a Java Program that demonstrates thread priority. Create two threads with different priorities and observe their execution order.**

Code-

```
public class ThreadPriorityDemo {
    public static void main(String[] args) {
        Runnable task = () ->{
            for (int i = 1; i <= 5; i++) {
                System.out.println(Thread.currentThread().getName() + ": " + i);
            }
        };

        Thread thread1 = new Thread(task);
        Thread thread2 = new Thread(task);

        thread1.setPriority(Thread.MIN_PRIORITY); // Priority 1
        thread2.setPriority(Thread.MAX_PRIORITY); // Priority 10

        thread1.start();
        thread2.start();
    }
}
```

Output-

```
Thread-0: 1
Thread-0: 2
Thread-0: 3
Thread-0: 4
Thread-0: 5
Thread-1: 1
Thread-1: 2
Thread-1: 3
Thread-1: 4
Thread-1: 5
```

4. **Write a Java Program that demonstrates thread communication using wait() and notify(). Create two threads, one to print odd numbers and the other to print even numbers in sequence.**

Code-

```
public class OddEvenThreadDemo {
    private static Object lock = new Object();
    private static int count = 1;
```

```
public static void main(String[] args) {
   Runnable oddTask = () -> {
      synchronized (lock) {
         while (count <= 10) {
            if (count % 2 != 0) {
               System.out.println(Thread.currentThread().getName() + ": " + count);
               count++;
               lock.notify();
            } else {
try {
                  lock.wait();
               } catch (InterruptedException e) {
                  e.printStackTrace();
               }
            }
         }
      }
   };

Runnable evenTask = () -> {
      synchronized (lock) {
         while (count <= 10) {
            if (count % 2 == 0) {
               System.out.println(Thread.currentThread().getName() + ": " + count);
  count++;
               lock.notify();
            } else {
               try {
                  lock.wait();
               } catch (InterruptedException e) {
                  e.printStackTrace();
               }
            }
         }
      }
   };

   Thread oddThread = new Thread(oddTask, "OddThread");
   Thread evenThread = new Thread(evenTask, "EvenThread");
```

```
        oddThread.start();
        evenThread.start();
    }
}
```

Output -

OddThread: 1
EvenThread: 2
OddThread: 3
EvenThread: 4
OddThread: 5
EvenThread: 6
OddThread: 7
EvenThread: 8
OddThread: 9
EvenThread: 10

5. Write a Java Program that demonstrates the use of the Thread class to create multiple threads.

Code-

```
public class ThreadDemo {
    public static void main(String[] args) {
        Thread thread1 = new Thread(() -> {
            System.out.println("Thread 1: Hello from Thread 1");
        });
        Thread thread2 = new Thread(() -> {
            System.out.println("Thread 2: Hello from Thread 2");
        });
        Thread thread3 = new Thread(() -> {
            System.out.println("Thread 3: Hello from Thread 3");
        });

        thread1.start();
        thread2.start();
        thread3.start();
    }
}
```

Output-

Thread 1: Hello from Thread 1
Thread 2: Hello from Thread 2

Thread 3: Hello from Thread 3

6. Create a Java Program that demonstrates the use of the synchronized keyword for method-level synchronization. Define a class with a synchronized method, and two threads that access it concurrently.

Code-

```
class SynchronizedMethodDemo {
    synchronized void printNumbers() {
        for (int i = 1; i <= 5; i++) {
            System.out.println(Thread.currentThread().getName() + ": " + i);
        }
    }

    public static void main(String[] args) {
        SynchronizedMethodDemo demo = new SynchronizedMethodDemo();

        Thread thread1 = new Thread(() -> {
            demo.printNumbers();
        });

        Thread thread2 = new Thread(() -> {
            demo.printNumbers();
        });

  thread1.start();
        thread2.start();
    }
}
```

Output:

The output will show that the threads execute the synchronized method one after the other, not concurrently.

7. Write a Java Program that demonstrates the use of the volatile keyword. Create a shared variable and two threads that read and modify its value concurrently.

Code-

```
public class VolatileDemo {
    private volatile int sharedValue = 0;

    public void incrementValue() {
        sharedValue++;
```

```
    }

    public static void main(String[] args) {
        VolatileDemo demo = new VolatileDemo();

        Thread thread1 = new Thread(() -> {
            for (int i = 0; i < 1000; i++) {
                demo.incrementValue();
            }
        });

    Thread thread2 = new Thread(() -> {
            for (int i = 0; i < 1000; i++) {
                demo.incrementValue();
            }
        });

        thread1.start();
        thread2.start();

        try {
            thread1.join();
            thread2.join();
        } catch (InterruptedException e) {
            e.printStackTrace();
        }

        System.out.println("Shared Value: " + demo.sharedValue);
    }
}
```

Output-

Shared Value: 1975

8. Create a Java Program that demonstrates the use of the ExecutorService framework. Implement a thread pool and submit tasks to it to perform concurrent operations.

Code-

```
import java.util.concurrent.ExecutorService;
import java.util.concurrent.Executors;

public class ThreadPoolDemo {
```

```
    public static void main(String[] args) {
        ExecutorService executor = Executors.newFixedThreadPool(3);

        Runnable task1 = () -> {
            System.out.println("Task 1: Executed by " + Thread.currentThread().getName());
        };

        Runnable task2 = () -> {
            System.out.println("Task 2: Executed by " + Thread.currentThread().getName());
        };

        Runnable task3 = () -> {
            System.out.println("Task 3: Executed by " + Thread.currentThread().getName());
        };

        executor.execute(task1);
        executor.execute(task2);
        executor.execute(task3);

        executor.shutdown();
    }
}
```

Output-

```
Task 2: Executed by pool-1-thread-2
Task 1: Executed by pool-1-thread-1
Task 3: Executed by pool-1-thread-3
```

9. Write a Java Program that demonstrates deadlock. Create two threads that lock resources in a way that leads to a deadlock situation.

Code-

```
public class DeadlockDemo {
    private static final Object resource1 = new Object();
    private static final Object resource2 = new Object();

    public static void main(String[] args) {
        Thread thread1 = new Thread(() -> {
            synchronized (resource1) {
                System.out.println("Thread 1: Locked resource 1");
                try {
                    Thread.sleep(100);
```

```
            } catch (InterruptedException e) {
                e.printStackTrace();
            }
            System.out.println("Thread 1: Waiting for resource 2");
            synchronized (resource2) {
                System.out.println("Thread 1: Locked resource 2");
            }
        }
    });

    Thread thread2 = new Thread(() -> {
        synchronized (resource2) {
            System.out.println("Thread 2: Locked resource 2");
            try {
                Thread.sleep(100);
            } catch (InterruptedException e) {
                e.printStackTrace();
            }
            System.out.println("Thread 2: Waiting for resource 1");
            synchronized (resource1) {
                System.out.println("Thread 2: Locked resource 1");
        }
        }
    });

    thread1.start();
    thread2.start();
  }
}
```

Output-

Thread 1: Locked resource 1Thread 2: Locked resource 2Thread 1: Waiting for resource 2
Thread 2: Waiting for resource 1

10. Create a Java Program that demonstrates the use of wait() and notify() for thread communication. Implement a producer-consumer scenario with two threads, one producing items and the other consuming them.

Code-

```
public class ThreadCommunication {
  private static final Object lock = new Object();
  private static boolean helloPrinted = false;
```

```
    public static void main(String[] args) {
        Runnable helloTask = () -> {
            synchronized (lock) {
                System.out.println("Hello");
                helloPrinted = true;
                lock.notify();
            }
        };

        Runnable worldTask = () -> {
            synchronized (lock) {
                while (!helloPrinted) {
                    try {
                        lock.wait();
                    } catch (InterruptedException e) {
                        e.printStackTrace();
                    }
                }
                System.out.println("World");
            }
        };

Thread thread1 = new Thread(helloTask);
        Thread thread2 = new Thread(worldTask);

        thread1.start();
        thread2.start();
    }
}
```

Output –

Hello
World

11. Create a Java Program that demonstrates thread local variables. Define a thread-local variable to store user session data, and create multiple threads to access and modify their own thread-local values.

Code-

```
public class ThreadLocalDemo {
    private static ThreadLocal<Integer> sessionData = ThreadLocal.withInitial(() -> 0);
```

```
    public static void main(String[] args) {
        Runnable task = () -> {
            int value = sessionData.get();
            System.out.println(Thread.currentThread().getName() + ": Session Data = " + value);
            sessionData.set(value + 1);
        };

        Thread thread1 = new Thread(task, "Thread A");
        Thread thread2 = new Thread(task, "Thread B");

        thread1.start();
        thread2.start();
    }
}
```

Output-

Thread A: Session Data = 0
Thread B: Session Data = 0

12. Write a Java Program that demonstrates the use of ExecutorService to manage a thread pool. Create a thread pool with a fixed number of threads and submit multiple tasks for execution.

Code-

```
import java.util.concurrent.ExecutorService;
import java.util.concurrent.Executors;

public class ThreadPoolDemo {
    public static void main(String[] args) {
        ExecutorService executorService = Executors.newFixedThreadPool(3);

        Runnable task = () -> {
            System.out.println(Thread.currentThread().getName() + ": Task executed.");
        };

        for (int i = 0; i < 5; i++) {
            executorService.submit(task);
        }

        executorService.shutdown();
    }
```

}

Output-

pool-1-thread-2: Task executed.
pool-1-thread-1: Task executed.
pool-1-thread-1: Task executed.
pool-1-thread-1: Task executed.
pool-1-thread-3: Task executed.

Practise Questions

1. Write a Java Program that demonstrates thread starvation. Create three threads with different priorities and a shared resource. One thread has a high priority and constantly accesses the resource, while the others have lower priorities. Explain how thread starvation occurs.
2. Create a Java Program that demonstrates the use of the volatile keyword. Define two threads, one to write to a volatile variable and another to read from it. Show how the volatile keyword ensures visibility of changes between threads.
3. Write a Java Program that demonstrates the use of the ThreadLocalRandom class. Create multiple threads that generate random numbers independently using ThreadLocalRandom and print them.
4. Create a Java Program that demonstrates the use of ExecutorService with a fixed thread pool. Define a task that simulates a database connection, and submit multiple tasks concurrently to the thread pool to observe parallel execution.
5. Write a Java Program that demonstrates deadlock avoidance using the tryLock() method of the ReentrantLock class. Create two threads that access two locks in a specific order, and if a lock is not available, use tryLock() to avoid deadlock.
6. Create a Java Program that demonstrates the use of the ReadWriteLock interface for concurrent reading and writing access to a shared resource. Define multiple reader and writer threads and show how read operations can occur simultaneously.
7. Write a Java Program that demonstrates thread interruption. Create a long-running task in a thread and interrupt it from another thread. Handle the interruption and terminate the long-running task gracefully.
8. Create a Java Program that demonstrates the use of a CountDownLatch to wait for multiple threads to complete their tasks before continuing. Define three worker threads that perform tasks and wait for them to finish.
9. Write a Java Program that demonstrates the use of the Phaser class to synchronize threads. Define multiple threads that register with a phaser and execute tasks in different phases.
10. Create a Java Program that demonstrates the use of Semaphore for limiting access to a shared resource. Define multiple threads that try to access the resource, and set a limit using a semaphore. Explain how the semaphore controls access.

1. Write a Java Program that demonstrates the use of generics with an ArrayList to store and retrieve elements of different data types (e.g., integers, strings).

Code-

```
import java.util.ArrayList;

public class GenericArrayListExample {
   public static void main(String[] args) {
      ArrayList<Integer> intList = new ArrayList<>();
      intList.add(42);

      ArrayList<String> strList = new ArrayList<>();
      strList.add("Hello, Generics!");

      System.out.println("Integer List: " + intList.get(0));
      System.out.println("String List: " + strList.get(0));
   }
}
```

Output-

```
Integer List: 42
String List: Hello, Generics!
```

2. Write a Java Program that defines a generic method to find the maximum element in an array of any data type (e.g., integers, doubles).

Code-

```
public class GenericMaxFinder {
   public static <T extends Comparable<T>> T findMax(T[] arr) {
      T max = arr[0];
      for (T element : arr) {
         if (element.compareTo(max) > 0) {
        max = element;
         }
      }
      return max;
   }

   public static void main(String[] args) {
      Integer[] intArr = {3, 7, 2, 9, 5};
      Double[] doubleArr = {3.14, 1.518, 2.708, 0.677};
```

```
        System.out.println("Maximum Integer: " + findMax(intArr));
        System.out.println("Maximum Double: " + findMax(doubleArr));
    }
}
```

Output-

Maximum Integer: 9
Maximum Double: 3.14

3. **Write a Java Program that uses generics to create a HashMap where the keys are strings and the values are integers. Add key-value pairs and retrieve values based on keys.**

Code-

```
import java.util.HashMap;

public class GenericHashMapExample {
    public static void main(String[] args) {
        HashMap<String, Integer> scores = new HashMap<>();
        scores.put("Aliya", 95);
        scores.put("Rakhi", 88);
        scores.put("Charlie", 92);

        System.out.println("Rakhi's Score: " + scores.get("Rakhi"));
    }
}
```

Output -

Rakhi's Score: 88

4. **Write a Java Program that demonstrates the use of generics with a linked list (LinkedList) to store and retrieve elements of different data types (e.g., strings, booleans).**

Code-

```
import java.util.LinkedList;

public class GenericLinkedListExample {
    public static void main(String[] args) {
        LinkedList<String> strList = new LinkedList<>();
        strList.add("Java");
        strList.add("is");
        strList.add("fun!");
```

```
        LinkedList<Boolean> boolList = new LinkedList<>();
        boolList.add(true);
        boolList.add(false);

        System.out.println("String List: " + String.join(" ", strList));
        System.out.println("Boolean List: " + boolList);
    }
}
```

Output -

String List: Java is fun!

Boolean List: [true, false]

5. Write a Java Program that uses wildcards <?> to print the elements of a generic collection without knowing the exact type.

Code-

```
import java.util.ArrayList;

public class WildcardExample {
    public static void printElements(ArrayList<?> list) {
     for (Object element : list) {
            System.out.print(element + " ");
        }
        System.out.println();
    }

    public static void main(String[] args) {
        ArrayList<Integer> intList = new ArrayList<>();
        intList.add(1);
    intList.add(2);
        intList.add(3);

        ArrayList<String> strList = new ArrayList<>();
        strList.add("Hello");
        strList.add("Generics!");

        printElements(intList);
        printElements(strList);
    }
}
```

Output -

12 3

Hello Generics!

6. Create a Java Program for accessing values in a HashMap.

Code-

```
import java.util.HashMap;

public class HashMapExample2 {
   public static void main(String[] args) {
      HashMap<String, Integer> hashMap = new HashMap<>();
hashMap.put("Aliya", 15);
      hashMap.put("Rakhi", 20);

      int age = hashMap.get("Aliya");
      System.out.println("Aliya age is: " + age);
   }
}
```

Output-

Aliya age is: 15

7. Create a Java Program to remove Key-Value Pairs from a HashMap.

Code-

```
import java.util.HashMap;

public class HashMapExample3 {
   public static void main(String[] args) {
      HashMap<String, Integer> hashMap = new HashMap<>();
      hashMap.put("Aliya", 25);
      hashMap.put("Rakhi", 30);

      hashMap.remove("Rakhi");
      System.out.println(hashMap);
   }
}


import java.util.HashMap;
import java.util.Map;
```

```
public class HashMapExample4 {
    public static void main(String[] args) {
        HashMap<String, Integer> hashMap = new HashMap<>();
        hashMap.put("Aliya", 25);
        hashMap.put("Rakhi", 30);

        for (Map.Entry<String, Integer> entry : hashMap.entrySet()) {
            System.out.println(entry.getKey() + ": " + entry.getValue());
        }
    }
}
```

Output-

Rakhi: 30
Aliya: 25

8. Create a Java Program to check if a Key Exists in a HashMap.

Code-

```
import java.util.HashMap;

public class HashMapExample5 {
    public static void main(String[] args) {
        HashMap<String, Integer> hashMap = new HashMap<>();
        hashMap.put("Aliya", 25);
        hashMap.put("Rakhi", 30);

        boolean containsKey = hashMap.containsKey("Aliya");
        System.out.println("Contains Aliya? " + containsKey);
    }
}
```

Output-

Contains Aliya? true

9. Create a Java Program for getting the size of a HashMap.

Code-

```
import java.util.HashMap;

public class HashMapExample6 {
    public static void main(String[] args) {
        HashMap<String, Integer> hashMap = new HashMap<>();
        hashMap.put("Aliya", 25);
```

```
        hashMap.put("Rakhi", 30);

        int size = hashMap.size();
        System.out.println("Size of HashMap: " + size);
    }
}
```

Output-

Size of HashMap: 2

10. Create a Java Program to check Hashmap is empty or not.

Code-

```
import java.util.HashMap;

public class HashMapExample7 {
    public static void main(String[] args) {
        HashMap<String, Integer> hashMap = new HashMap<>();

        boolean isEmpty = hashMap.isEmpty();
        System.out.println("Is HashMap empty? " + isEmpty);
    }
}
```

Output-

Is HashMap empty? True

11. Create a Java Program for copying a HashMap.

Code-

```
import java.util.HashMap;

public class HashMapExample8 {
    public static void main(String[] args) {
        HashMap<String, Integer> originalHashMap = new HashMap<>();
        originalHashMap.put("Aliya", 25);
        originalHashMap.put("Rakhi", 30);

        HashMap<String, Integer> copiedHashMap = new HashMap<>(originalHashMap);
        System.out.println("Copied HashMap: " + copiedHashMap);
    }
}
```

Output-

Copied HashMap: {Rakhi=30, Aliya=25}

12. Create a Java Program to clear a HashMap.

Code-

```
import java.util.HashMap;

public class HashMapExample9 {
    public static void main(String[] args) {
        HashMap<String, Integer> hashMap = new HashMap<>();
        hashMap.put("Aliya", 25);
        hashMap.put("Rakhi", 30);

        hashMap.clear();
        System.out.println("HashMap after clearing: " + hashMap);
    }
}
```

Output-

```
HashMap after clearing: {}
```

13. Write a Java Program that demonstrates the use of a generic class to create a stack (using ArrayList) that can store elements of any data type. Push elements onto the stack, pop them, and print the result.

Code-

```
import java.util.ArrayList;

public class GenericStack<T> {
    private ArrayList<T> stack = new ArrayList<>();

    public void push(T element) {
        stack.add(element);
    }

    public T pop() {
        if (!stack.isEmpty()) {
            return stack.remove(stack.size() - 1);
        }
        return null;
    }

    public static void main(String[] args) {
        GenericStack<Integer> intStack = new GenericStack<>();
```

```
        intStack.push(1);
        intStack.push(2);
 System.out.println("Popped Integer: " + intStack.pop());

        GenericStack<String> strStack = new GenericStack<>();
        strStack.push("Hello");
        strStack.push("Generics!");
        System.out.println("Popped String: " + strStack.pop());
    }
}
```

Output-

Popped Integer: 2

Popped String: Generics!

14. Create a Java Program that demonstrates the use of the enhanced for loop (for-each loop) with a generic ArrayList. Define an ArrayList with elements of any data type and print them using the for-each loop.

Code-

```
import java.util.ArrayList;

public class GenericArrayListLoop {
    public static void main(String[] args) {
        ArrayList<Object> myList = new ArrayList<>();
        myList.add(42);
        myList.add("Hello, Generics!");
        myList.add(3.14);

        for (Object element : myList) {
         System.out.println(element);
        }
    }
}
```

Output-

42

Hello, Generics!

3.14

15. Write a Java program that demonstrates the use of a generic method to reverse the elements of an ArrayList. Define a generic method to reverse the order of elements in the ArrayList and print the result.

Code-

```
import java.util.ArrayList;

public class GenericArrayListReverse {
    public static <T> void reverseArrayList(ArrayList<T> list) {
        int left = 0;
        int right = list.size() - 1;
        while (left < right) {
            T temp = list.get(left);
            list.set(left, list.get(right));
            list.set(right, temp);
            left++;
            right--;
        }
    }

    public static void main(String[] args) {
    ArrayList<Integer> intList = new ArrayList<>();
        intList.add(1);
        intList.add(2);
        intList.add(3);

        ArrayList<String> strList = new ArrayList<>();
        strList.add("Java");
        strList.add("is");
        strList.add("fun!");

        reverseArrayList(intList);
        reverseArrayList(strList);

        System.out.println("Reversed Integer List: " + intList);
        System.out.println("Reversed String List: " + strList);
    }
}
```

Output-

Reversed Integer List: [3, 2, 1]

Reversed String List: [fun!, is, Java]

16. Create a Java Program that demonstrates the use of a generic class to implement a key-value pair. Define a generic class to represent key-value pairs and store them in a HashMap. Print the key-value pairs.

Code-

```
import java.util.HashMap;

class KeyValuePair<K, V> {
    private K key;
    private V value;

    public KeyValuePair(K key, V value) {
        this.key = key;
        this.value = value;
    }

    public K getKey() {
        return key;
    }

    public V getValue() {
        return value;
    }
}

public class GenericKeyValuePairDemo {
    public static void main(String[] args) {
        HashMap<String, Integer> map = new HashMap<>();
        KeyValuePair<String, Integer> pair1 = new KeyValuePair<>("One", 1);
        KeyValuePair<String, Integer> pair2 = new KeyValuePair<>("Two", 2);

        map.put(pair1.getKey(), pair1.getValue());
        map.put(pair2.getKey(), pair2.getValue());

        for (String key : map.keySet()) {
            System.out.println(key + ": " + map.get(key));
        }
    }
}
```

Output-

One: 1

Two: 2

17. Write a Java Program that demonstrates the use of a generic method to count the occurrences of an element in an ArrayList. Define a generic method to count occurrences and print the result.

Code-

```
import java.util.ArrayList;

public class GenericElementCounter {
    public static <T> int countOccurrences(ArrayList<T> list, T target) {
        int count = 0;
        for (T element : list) {
            if (element.equals(target)) {
                count++;
            }
        }
        return count;
    }

    public static void main(String[] args) {
        ArrayList<String> strList = new ArrayList<>();
        strList.add("apple");
        strList.add("banana");
        strList.add("apple");
        strList.add("cherry");
        strList.add("apple");

        int appleCount = countOccurrences(strList, "apple");
        int bananaCount = countOccurrences(strList, "banana");

        System.out.println("Occurrences of 'apple': " + appleCount);
        System.out.println("Occurrences of 'banana': " + bananaCount);
    }
}
```

Output-

Occurrences of 'apple': 3

Occurrences of 'banana': 1

18. Create a Java Program that demonstrates the use of a generic wildcard (?) to accept collections of different generic types. Define a method to print the elements of any collection without knowing its generic type.

Code-

```
import java.util.ArrayList;
import java.util.LinkedList;

public class GenericWildcardDemo {
  public static void printElements(ArrayList<?> list) {
    for (Object element : list) {
      System.out.print(element + " ");
    }
    System.out.println();
  }

  public static void main(String[] args) {
    ArrayList<Integer> intList = new ArrayList<>();
    intList.add(1);
    intList.add(2);
    intList.add(3);

    LinkedList<String> strList = new LinkedList<>();
    strList.add("Hello");
    strList.add("Generics!");

    printElements(intList);
    printElements(strList);
  }
}
```

Output-

```
1 2 3
Hello Generics!
```

19. Write a Java Program that demonstrates the use of a generic class to create a queue (using LinkedList) that can store elements of any data type. Enqueue and dequeue elements from the queue and print the result.

Code-

```
import java.util.LinkedList;
```

```
public class GenericQueue<T> {
   private LinkedList<T> queue = new LinkedList<>();

   public void enqueue(T element) {
      queue.addLast(element);
   }

   public T dequeue() {
      if (!queue.isEmpty()) {
         return queue.removeFirst();
   }
      return null;
   }

   public static void main(String[] args) {
      GenericQueue<Integer> intQueue = new GenericQueue<>();
      intQueue.enqueue(1);
      intQueue.enqueue(2);
      System.out.println("Dequeued Integer: " + intQueue.dequeue());

      GenericQueue<String> strQueue = new GenericQueue<>();
      strQueue.enqueue("Hello");
      strQueue.enqueue("Generics!");
      System.out.println("Dequeued String: " + strQueue.dequeue());
   }
}
```

Output-

Dequeued Integer: 1
Dequeued String: Hello

20. Create a Java Program that demonstrates the use of a generic method to find the minimum element in an array of any data type (e.g., integers, doubles).

Code-

```
public class GenericMinFinder {
   public static <T extends Comparable<T>> T findMin(T[] arr) {
      T min = arr[0];
      for (T element : arr) {
         if (element.compareTo(min) < 0) {
            min = element;
```

```
        }
      }
      return min;
    }

    public static void main(String[] args) {
      Integer[] intArr = {3, 7, 2, 9, 5};
      Double[] doubleArr = {3.14, 1.518, 2.708, 0.677};

      System.out.println("Minimum Integer: " + findMin(intArr));
      System.out.println("Minimum Double: " + findMin(doubleArr));
    }
}
```

Output-

Minimum Integer: 2
Minimum Double: 0.677

21. Write a Java Program that demonstrates the use of a generic method to merge two ArrayLists of any data type into one ArrayList. Define a generic method to merge and print the result.

Code-

```
import java.util.ArrayList;

public class GenericArrayListMerger {
    public static <T> ArrayList<T> mergeArrayLists(ArrayList<T> list1, ArrayList<T> list2) {
      ArrayList<T> mergedList = new ArrayList<>();
      mergedList.addAll(list1);
      mergedList.addAll(list2);
      return mergedList;
    }

    public static void main(String[] args) {
      ArrayList<String> list1 = new ArrayList<>();
      list1.add("Java");
      list1.add("is");

      ArrayList<String> list2 = new ArrayList<>();
      list2.add("fun!");
      list2.add("Generics!");
```

```
        ArrayList<String> mergedList = mergeArrayLists(list1, list2);
        System.out.println("Merged ArrayList: " + mergedList);
    }
}
```

Output-

Merged ArrayList: [Java, is, fun!, Generics!]

22. Create a Java Program that demonstrates the use of a generic method to check, if an element exists in an ArrayList of any data type. Define a generic method to check existence and print the result.

Code-

```
import java.util.ArrayList;

public class GenericElementExistence {
    public static <T> boolean elementExists(ArrayList<T> list, T target) {
        return list.contains(target);
    }

    public static void main(String[] args) {
        ArrayList<Integer> intList = new ArrayList<>();
        intList.add(1);
        intList.add(2);
        intList.add(3);

        ArrayList<String> strList = new ArrayList<>();
        strList.add("Java");
        strList.add("is");
        strList.add("fun!");

        boolean existsInIntList = elementExists(intList, 2);
        boolean existsInStrList = elementExists(strList, "Generics!");

        System.out.println("Element '2' exists in Integer List: " + existsInIntList);
        System.out.println("Element 'Generics!' exists in String List: " + existsInStrList);
    }
}
```

Output-

Element '2' exists in Integer List: true
Element 'Generics!' exists in String List: true

Practise Questions

1. Write a Java Program that demonstrates the use of a generic class to implement a linked list (using LinkedList) that can store elements of any data type. Add elements to the linked list, remove elements, and print the final list.
2. Create a Java Program that demonstrates the use of a generic method to find the average of elements in an ArrayList of integers.
3. Write a Java Program that demonstrates the use of a generic class to implement a binary tree that can store elements of any data type. Insert elements into the tree, perform an in-order traversal, and print the sorted elements.
4. Create a Java Program that demonstrates the use of a generic class to implement a queue (using LinkedList) that can store elements of any data type. Enqueue elements, dequeue them, and print the dequeued elements.
5. Write a Java Program that demonstrates the use of a generic method to merge two ArrayLists of different data types into one ArrayList. Define a generic method to merge and print the merged ArrayList.
6. Create a Java Program that demonstrates the use of a generic method to find the maximum element in an ArrayList of any data type (e.g., integers, doubles).
7. Write a Java Program that demonstrates the use of wildcards to print the elements of a generic ArrayList without knowing the exact type. Define a method to print the elements using wildcards.
8. Create a Java Program that demonstrates the use of a generic class to implement a stack (using ArrayList) that can store elements of any data type. Push elements onto the stack, pop them, and print the popped elements.
9. Write a Java Program that demonstrates the use of a generic class to implement a priority queue (using PriorityQueue) that can store elements of any data type. Add elements to the priority queue with different priorities and print them in the order they are dequeued.
10. Create a Java Program that demonstrates the use of a generic method to reverse the elements in an ArrayList of any data type. Define a generic method to reverse the list and print the reversed list.

1. Write a Java Program that demonstrates basic string operations such as concatenation and length calculation.

Code-

```
public class StringBasics {
    public static void main(String[] args) {
        String firstName = "Jai";
        String lastName = "Gupta";
        String fullName = firstName + " " + lastName;
        int length = fullName.length();

        System.out.println("Full Name: " + fullName);
        System.out.println("Length of Full Name: " + length);
    }
}
```

Output -

Full Name: Jay Gupta
Length of Full Name: 8

2. Write a Java Program that compares two strings to check, if they are equal (case-sensitive) and, if they are equal ignoring case.

Code-

```
public class StringComparison {
    public static void main(String[] args) {
        String str1 = "Hello, World!";
        String str2 = "hello, world!";

        boolean caseSensitiveEquality = str1.equals(str2);
        boolean caseInsensitiveEquality = str1.equalsIgnoreCase(str2);

        System.out.println("Case-Sensitive Equality: " + caseSensitiveEquality);
        System.out.println("Case-Insensitive Equality: " + caseInsensitiveEquality);
    }
}
```

Output -

Case-Sensitive Equality: false
Case-Insensitive Equality: true

3. Write a Java Program that splits a sentence into words using the split method and displays them.

Code-

```
public class StringSplitting {
   public static void main(String[] args) {
      String sentence = "Java programming is fun";
      String[] words = sentence.split(" ");

      System.out.println("Words in the Sentence:");
      for (String word : words) {
         System.out.println(word);
      }
   }
}
```

Output-

Words in the Sentence:

Java programming is fun

4. Write a Java Program that formats a date string in different ways using String format.

Code-

```
public class StringFormatting {
   public static void main(String[] args) {
      int day = 10;
      int month = 6;
      int year = 2023;

      String formattedDate1 = String.format("%02d-%02d-%04d", day, month, year);
      String formattedDate2 = String.format("%d/%d/%02d", month, day, year % 100);

      System.out.println("Formatted Date 1: " + formattedDate1);
      System.out.println("Formatted Date 2: " + formattedDate2);
   }
}
```

Output –

Formatted Date 1: 10-06-2023

Formatted Date 2: 6/10/23

5. Write a Java Program that searches for a substring within a string using the indexOf method.

Code-

```
public class StringSearching {
    public static void main(String[] args) {
        String text = "Java is a powerful programming language";
        String searchTerm = "powerful";

        int index = text.indexOf(searchTerm);

        if (index != -1) {
            System.out.println("Found the search term at index: " + index);
        } else {
            System.out.println("Search term not found.");
        }
    }
}
```

Output-

Found the search term at index: 10

6. Create an enumeration called "DayOfWeek" to represent days of the week. Write a program that prints all the days using the enumeration.

Code-

```
public enum DayOfWeek {
    SUNDAY, MONDAY, TUESDAY, WEDNESDAY, THURSDAY, FRIDAY, SATURDAY
}

public class EnumExample {
    public static void main(String[] args) {
        for (DayOfWeek day : DayOfWeek.values()) {
            System.out.println(day);
        }
    }
}
```

Output-

SUNDAY
MONDAY
TUESDAY
WEDNESDAY
THURSDAY
FRIDAY
SATURDAY

7. Create an enumeration called "Season" to represent seasons (e.g., SPRING, SUMMER). Write a program that asks the user for their favourite season and displays a message accordingly.

Code-

```
import java.util.Scanner;

public enum Season {
   SPRING, SUMMER, AUTUMN, WINTER
}

public class FavouriteSeason {
   public static void main(String[] args) {
      Scanner scanner = new Scanner(System.in);
      System.out.print("Enter your favourite season: ");
      String input = scanner.nextLine().toUpperCase();

      try {
         Season favouriteSeason = Season.valueOf(input);
         System.out.println("Your favourite season is " + favouriteSeason);
      } catch (IllegalArgumentException e) {
         System.out.println("Invalid season entered.");
      }
   }
}
```

Output-

Enter your favourite season: SUMMER
Your favourite season is SUMMER

8. Create a custom annotation called "MethodInfo" with attributes for method name and author. Write a program that uses this annotation to annotate a method and then displays the method information.

Code-

```
import java.lang.annotation.*;

@Retention(RetentionPolicy.RUNTIME)
@Target(ElementType.METHOD)
@interface MethodInfo {
   String methodName();
   String author();
```

```
}

public class CustomAnnotationExample {
   @MethodInfo(methodName = "printHello", author = "John Doe")
   public static void printHello() {
      System.out.println("Hello, Custom Annotation!");
   }

   public static void main(String[] args) {
      try {
         Class<?> clazz = CustomAnnotationExample.class;
         Method method = clazz.getMethod("printHello");

         MethodInfo annotation = method.getAnnotation(MethodInfo.class);
         System.out.println("Method Name: " + annotation.methodName());
         System.out.println("Author: " + annotation.author());
      } catch (NoSuchMethodException e) {
         e.printStackTrace();
      }
   }
}
```

Output-

```
Method Name: printHello
Author: John Doe
```

9. Write a program that uses lambda expressions to sort a list of strings in ascending order.

Code-

```
import java.util.ArrayList;
import java.util.Collections;
import java.util.List;

public class LambdaSortingExample {
   public static void main(String[] args) {
      List<String> fruits = new ArrayList<>();
     fruits.add("Apple");
      fruits.add("Banana");
      fruits.add("Cherry");
      fruits.add("Date");

      Collections.sort(fruits, (s1, s2) -> s1.compareTo(s2));
```

```
        System.out.println("Sorted Fruits: " + fruits);
    }
}
```

Output-

Sorted Fruits: [Apple, Banana, Cherry, Date]

10. Write a program that uses lambda expressions to find the square of each element in an integer list.

Code-

```
import java.util.ArrayList;
import java.util.List;

public class LambdaSquareExample {
    public static void main(String[] args) {
        List<Integer> numbers = new ArrayList<>();
        numbers.add(1);
        numbers.add(2);
        numbers.add(3);
        numbers.add(4);

        numbers.forEach((n) -> System.out.println(n * n));
}
}
```

Output -

1
4
9
16

11. Write a program that demonstrates the use of a Queue to implement a simple task queue. Add tasks to the queue and process them in a FIFO manner.

Code-

```
import java.util.LinkedList;
import java.util.Queue;

public class TaskQueueExample {
    public static void main(String[] args) {
```

```
        Queue<String> taskQueue = new LinkedList<>();

        // Adding tasks to the queue
        taskQueue.offer("Task 1");
        taskQueue.offer("Task 2");
        taskQueue.offer("Task 3");

        // Processing tasks in FIFO order
        while (!taskQueue.isEmpty()) {
            System.out.println("Processing: " + taskQueue.poll());
        }
    }
}
```

Output:

Processing: Task 1
Processing: Task 2
Processing: Task 3

12. Write a program that uses a HashMap to store and retrieve student names and their corresponding scores.

Display the names and scores in alphabetical order of the names.

Code-

```
import java.util.HashMap;
import java.util.Map;
import java.util.TreeMap;

public class StudentScoresExample {
    public static void main(String[] args) {
        Map<String, Integer> studentScores = new HashMap<>();

        studentScores.put("Aliya", 85);
        studentScores.put("Rakhi", 92);
        studentScores.put("Charlie", 78);
        studentScores.put("David", 95);

        Map<String, Integer> sortedStudentScores = new TreeMap<>(studentScores);

        for (Map.Entry<String, Integer> entry : sortedStudentScores.entrySet()) {
            System.out.println(entry.getKey() + ": " + entry.getValue());
        }
```

```
    }
}
```

Output-

Aliya: 85
Rakhi: 92
Charlie: 78
David: 95

13. Write a program that demonstrates the use of a ConcurrentHashMap to safely store and update data by multiple threads.

Code-

```
import java.util.concurrent.ConcurrentHashMap;

public class ConcurrentMapExample {
  public static void main(String[] args) {
    ConcurrentHashMap<String, Integer> concurrentMap = new ConcurrentHashMap<>();

    concurrentMap.put("Key1", 10);
    concurrentMap.put("Key2", 20);

    Runnable task1 = () -> {
      concurrentMap.put("Key1", concurrentMap.get("Key1") + 5);
    };

    Runnable task2 = () -> {
      concurrentMap.put("Key2", concurrentMap.get("Key2") + 10);
    };

    Thread thread1 = new Thread(task1);
    Thread thread2 = new Thread(task2);

    thread1.start();
    thread2.start();

    try {
  thread1.join();
      thread2.join();
    } catch (InterruptedException e) {
      e.printStackTrace();
```

```
        }

        System.out.println("Updated values: " + concurrentMap);
    }
```

Output-

Updated values: {Key1=15, Key2=30}

14. Create a Java Program that demonstrates how to create and display a Linked List.

Code-

```
import java.util.LinkedList;

public class CreateAndDisplayLinkedList {
    public static void main(String[] args) {
        LinkedList<String> linkedList = new LinkedList<>();

        linkedList.add("Apple");
        linkedList.add("Banana");
        linkedList.add("Cherry");

        System.out.println("Linked List Elements:");
        for (String fruit : linkedList) {
            System.out.println(fruit);
        }
    }
}
```

Output-

Linked List Elements:
Apple
Banana
Cherry

15. Create a Java Program that demonstrates how to add and remove elements in a Linked List.

Code-

```
import java.util.LinkedList;

public class AddRemoveLinkedListElements {
    public static void main(String[] args) {
        LinkedList<Integer> linkedList = new LinkedList<>();
```

```
        linkedList.add(10);
        linkedList.add(20);
        linkedList.add(30);

        System.out.println("Linked List Elements: " + linkedList);

        linkedList.addFirst(5);
        linkedList.addLast(40);
        linkedList.remove(2);

        System.out.println("Modified Linked List: " + linkedList);
    }
}
```

Output-

Linked List Elements: [10, 20, 30]
Modified Linked List: [5, 10, 30, 40]

16. Create a Java Program that demonstrates how to reverse a Linked List.

Code-

```
import java.util.LinkedList;
import java.util.Collections;

public class ReverseLinkedList {
    public static void main(String[] args) {
        LinkedList<String> linkedList = new LinkedList<>();

        linkedList.add("Apple");
        linkedList.add("Banana");
        linkedList.add("Cherry");

        System.out.println("Original Linked List: " + linkedList);

        Collections.reverse(linkedList);

        System.out.println("Reversed Linked List: " + linkedList);
    }
}
```

Output-

Original Linked List: [Apple, Banana, Cherry]

Reversed Linked List: [Cherry, Banana, Apple]

17. Create a Java Program that demonstrates how to search for an element in a singly Linked List.

Code-

```
import java.util.LinkedList;

public class SearchLinkedListElement {
  public static void main(String[] args) {
    LinkedList<Integer> linkedList = new LinkedList<>();

    linkedList.add(10);
    linkedList.add(20);
    linkedList.add(30);

    int searchElement = 20;

    if (linkedList.contains(searchElement)) {
      System.out.println(searchElement + " found in the Linked List.");
    } else {
      System.out.println(searchElement + " not found in the Linked List.");
    }
  }
}
```

Output-

20 found in the Linked List.

18. Create a Java Program that demonstrates how to merge two Linked Lists.

Code-

```
import java.util.LinkedList;

public class MergeLinkedLists {
  public static void main(String[] args) {
    LinkedList<String> list1 = new LinkedList<>();
    list1.add("A");
    list1.add("B");

    LinkedList<String> list2 = new LinkedList<>();
    list2.add("C");
    list2.add("D");
```

```
        list1.addAll(list2);

        System.out.println("Merged Linked List: " + list1);
    }
}
```
Output-

Merged Linked List: [A, B, C, D]

19. Create a Java Program that demonstrates how to find a substring in a String.

Code-
```
public class SubstringSearch {
    public static void main(String[] args) {
        String text = "The quick brown fox jumps over the lazy dog.";
        String search = "fox";

        if (text.contains(search)) {
            System.out.println("Substring found!");
        } else {
            System.out.println("Substring not found.");
        }
    }
}
```
Output-

Substring found!

20. Create a Java Program that demonstrates how to reverse a String.

Code-
```
public class ReverseString {
    public static void main(String[] args) {
        String str = "Hello, World!";
        String reversed = new StringBuilder(str).reverse().toString();
      System.out.println("Reversed string: " + reversed);
    }
}
```
Output-

Reversed string: !dlroW ,olleH

21. Create a Java Program how to count the number of words in a sentence.

Code-

```
public class WordCount {
    public static void main(String[] args) {
        String sentence = "This is a sample sentence.";
        String[] words = sentence.split(" ");
        int wordCount = words.length;
        System.out.println("Word count: " + wordCount);
    }
}
```

Output-

Word count: 5

22. Write a Java Program that removes all white spaces from a given string.

Code-

```
public class RemoveWhiteSpace {
    public static void main(String[] args) {
        String input = "   Hello   World   ";
        String result = removeSpaces(input);
        System.out.println("String with spaces removed: \"" + result + "\"");
    }

    public static String removeSpaces(String str) {
        return str.replaceAll("\\s+", "");
    }
}
```

Output-

String with spaces removed: "HelloWorld"

Practise Questions

1. Write a Java Program that counts the occurrences of a specific character in a given string.
2. Write a Java Program that converts uppercase letters to lowercase and vice versa in a given string.
3. Write a Java Program that replaces a specific substring with another string in a given input.
4. Write a Java Program that finds the length of the longest word in a given sentence.
5. Write a Java Program that reverses the words in a given sentence.
6. Write a Java Program that checks if a given string starts or ends with a specific substring.
7. Write a Java Program that checks if a given substring exists within another string.

1. Write a Program that implements a custom stack data structure and performs push and pop operations.

Code-

```
import java.util.ArrayList;
import java.util.List;

class CustomStack<T> {
    private List<T> stack = new ArrayList<>();

    public void push(T item) {
        stack.add(item);
    }

    public T pop() {
        if (isEmpty()) {
        throw new IllegalStateException("Stack is empty");
        }
        return stack.remove(stack.size() - 1);
    }

    public boolean isEmpty() {
        return stack.isEmpty();
    }
}

public class CustomStackExample {
    public static void main(String[] args) {
        CustomStack<Integer> stack = new CustomStack<>();

        stack.push(3);
        stack.push(2);
        stack.push(1);

        while (!stack.isEmpty()) {
            System.out.println("Popped: " + stack.pop());
        }
    }
}
```

Output-

Popped: 1
Popped: 2
Popped: 3

2. Create a Java Program for merging two ArrayLists.

Code-

```
import java.util.ArrayList;
import java.util.Collections;

public class MergeArrayLists {
    public static void main(String[] args) {
        ArrayList<Integer> list1 = new ArrayList<>();
        list1.add(1);
        list1.add(2);

        ArrayList<Integer> list2 = new ArrayList<>();
        list2.add(3);
        list2.add(4);

        ArrayList<Integer> mergedList = new ArrayList<>();
        mergedList.addAll(list1);
        mergedList.addAll(list2);

        System.out.println("Merged ArrayList: " + mergedList);
    }
}
```

Output-

Merged ArrayList: [1, 2, 3, 4]

3. Create a Java Program for finding the maximum element in an array.

Code-

```
public class MaxArrayElement {
    public static void main(String[] args) {
        int[] arr = {10, 5, 20, 8, 15};
        int max = arr[0];

        for (int i = 1; i < arr.length; i++) {
            if (arr[i] > max) {
                max = arr[i];
```

```
            }
        }

        System.out.println("Maximum element in the array: " + max);
    }
}
```

Output-

Maximum element in the array: 20

4. Write a Java Program that calculates the sum of elements in an array.

Code-

```
public class SumArrayElements {
    public static void main(String[] args) {
        int[] arr = {10, 5, 20, 8, 15};
        int sum = 0;

        for (int num : arr) {
            sum += num;
    }

        System.out.println("Sum of elements in the array: " + sum);
    }
}
```

Output-

Sum of elements in the array: 58

5. Create a Java Program for copying elements from one array to another.

Code-

```
public class CopyArray {
    public static void main(String[] args) {
        int[] sourceArray = {1, 2, 3, 4, 5};
        int[] targetArray = new int[sourceArray.length];

        for (int i = 0; i < sourceArray.length; i++) {
            targetArray[i] = sourceArray[i];
        }

        System.out.print("Copied array: ");
        for (int num : targetArray) {
            System.out.print(num + " ");
```

```
        }
    }
}
```
Output-

Copied array: 1 2 3 4 5

6. Write a Java Program that reverses the elements of an array.

Code-

```
public class ReverseArray {
    public static void main(String[] args) {
        int[] arr = {1, 2, 3, 4, 5};
        int[] reversedArray = new int[arr.length];

        for (int i = 0, j = arr.length - 1; i < arr.length; i++, j--) {
            reversedArray[j] = arr[i];
        }

        System.out.print("Reversed array: ");
        for (int num : reversedArray) {
            System.out.print(num + " ");
        }
    }
}
```
Output-

Reversed array: 5 4 3 2 1

7. Write a Java Program that demonstrates how to iterate through the elements of an ArrayList.

Code-

```
import java.util.ArrayList;

public class IterateArrayList {
    public static void main(String[] args) {
        ArrayList<Integer> numbers = new ArrayList<>();

        numbers.add(10);
        numbers.add(20);
        numbers.add(30);
        numbers.add(40);
```

```
        System.out.println("Elements in the ArrayList:");
        for (int num : numbers) {
            System.out.println(num);
        }
    }
}
```

Output-
Elements in the ArrayList:
10
20
30
40

8. Write a Java Program that implements a custom queue data structure and performs enqueue and dequeue operations.

Code-

```
import java.util.LinkedList;
import java.util.List;

class CustomQueue<T> {
    private List<T> queue = new LinkedList<>();

    public void enqueue(T item) {
        queue.add(item);
    }

    public T dequeue() {
        if (isEmpty()) {
            throw new IllegalStateException("Queue is empty");
        }
        return queue.remove(0);
    }

    public boolean isEmpty() {
        return queue.isEmpty();
    }
}

public class CustomQueueExample {
```

```
    public static void main(String[] args) {
        CustomQueue<String> queue = new CustomQueue<>();

        queue.enqueue("A");
        queue.enqueue("B");
        queue.enqueue("C");

        while (!queue.isEmpty()) {
            System.out.println("Dequeued: " + queue.dequeue());
        }
    }
}
```

Output-

```
Dequeued: A
Dequeued: B
Dequeued: C
```

9. Write a Java Program that implements a custom HashSet data structure with add and contains operations.

Code-

```
import java.util.ArrayList;
import java.util.List;

class CustomHashSet<T> {
    private List<T> set = new ArrayList<>();

    public void add(T item) {
        if (!contains(item)) {
            set.add(item);
        }
    }

    public boolean contains(T item) {
        return set.contains(item);
    }

    public int size() {
        return set.size();
    }
}
```

```
public class CustomHashSetExample {
    public static void main(String[] args) {
        CustomHashSet<Integer> set = new CustomHashSet<>();

        set.add(1);
        set.add(2);
        set.add(3);
        set.add(1);

        System.out.println("Set size: " + set.size());
        System.out.println("Contains 2? " + set.contains(2));
        System.out.println("Contains 4? " + set.contains(4));
    }
}
```

Output-

```
Set size: 3
Contains 2? true
Contains 4? false
```

10. Write a Java Program that implements a custom singly linked list data structure with add and remove operations.

Code-

```
class CustomLinkedList<T> {
    private Node head;

    private class Node {
        T data;
        Node next;

        Node(T data) {
            this.data = data;
        }
    }

    public void add(T item) {
        Node newNode = new Node(item);
        newNode.next = head;
        head = newNode;
    }
```

```
    public void remove(T item) {
        if (head == null) {
            return;
        }
        if (head.data.equals(item)) {
            head = head.next;
            return;
        }

        Node current = head;
        while (current.next != null) {
            if (current.next.data.equals(item)) {
                current.next = current.next.next;
                return;
            }
            current = current.next;
        }
    }

    public void display() {
        Node current = head;
        while (current != null) {
            System.out.print(current.data + " ");
            current = current.next;
        }
        System.out.println();
    }
}

public class CustomLinkedListExample {
    public static void main(String[] args) {
        CustomLinkedList<Integer> list = new CustomLinkedList<>();

        list.add(1);
        list.add(2);
        list.add(3);
        list.display();

        list.remove(2);
```

```
        list.display();
    }
}
```

Output-

3 2 1

3 1

11. Write a Java Program that implements a custom stack data structure and performs push and pop operations.

Code-

```
import java.util.ArrayList;
import java.util.List;

class CustomStack<T> {
    private List<T> stack = new ArrayList<>();

    public void push(T item) {
        stack.add(item);
    }

    public T pop() {
        if (isEmpty()) {
            throw new IllegalStateException("Stack is empty");
        }
        return stack.remove(stack.size() - 1);
    }

    public boolean isEmpty() {
        return stack.isEmpty();
    }
}

public class CustomStackExample {
    public static void main(String[] args) {
        CustomStack<Integer> stack = new CustomStack<>();

        stack.push(3);
        stack.push(2);
        stack.push(1);
```

```
        while (!stack.isEmpty()) {
            System.out.println("Popped: " + stack.pop());
        }
    }
}
```

Output-

Popped: 1
Popped: 2
Popped: 3

12. Write a Java Program that implements a custom doubly linked list data structure with add and remove operations.

Code-

```
class CustomDoublyLinkedList<T> {
    private Node head;
    private Node tail;

    private class Node {
        T data;
        Node next;
        Node prev;

        Node(T data) {
            this.data = data;
        }
    }

    public void add(T item) {
       Node newNode = new Node(item);
        if (head == null) {
            head = newNode;
            tail = newNode;
        } else {
            newNode.prev = tail;
            tail.next = newNode;
            tail = newNode;
        }
    }

    public void remove(T item) {
```

```
        Node current = head;
        while (current != null) {
            if (current.data.equals(item)) {
                if (current == head) {
                    head = current.next;
                }
                if (current == tail) {
                    tail = current.prev;
                }
                if (current.prev != null) {
                    current.prev.next = current.next;
                }
                if (current.next != null) {
                    current.next.prev = current.prev;
                }
            }
            current = current.next;
        }
    }

    public void display() {
        Node current = head;
        while (current != null) {
            System.out.print(current.data + " ");
            current = current.next;
        }
        System.out.println();
    }
}

public class CustomDoublyLinkedListExample {
    public static void main(String[] args) {
        CustomDoublyLinkedList<Integer> list = new CustomDoublyLinkedList<>();

        list.add(1);
        list.add(2);
        list.add(3);
        list.display();

        list.remove(2);
```

```
        list.display();
    }
}
```

Output-

```
1 2 3
1 3
```

13. Write a Java Program that implements a custom priority queue data structure and performs enqueue and dequeue operations based on priority.

Code-

```
import java.util.ArrayList;
import java.util.List;

class CustomPriorityQueue<T extends Comparable<T>> {
    private List<T> queue = new ArrayList<>();

    public void enqueue(T item) {
        int index = 0;
        while (index < queue.size() && item.compareTo(queue.get(index)) > 0) {
            index++;
        }
        queue.add(index, item);
    }

    public T dequeue() {
        if (isEmpty()) {
            throw new IllegalStateException("Queue is empty");
        }
        return queue.remove(0);
    }

    public boolean isEmpty() {
        return queue.isEmpty();
    }
}

public class CustomPriorityQueueExample {
    public static void main(String[] args) {
        CustomPriorityQueue<Integer> queue = new CustomPriorityQueue<>();
```

```
        queue.enqueue(3);
        queue.enqueue(1);
        queue.enqueue(2);

        while (!queue.isEmpty()) {
            System.out.println("Dequeued: " + queue.dequeue());
        }
    }
}
```

Output-

Dequeued: 1
Dequeued: 2
Dequeued: 3

14. Write a Java Program that implements a custom binary search tree data structure with insert and search operations.

Code-

```
class Node<T extends Comparable<T>> {
    T data;
    Node<T> left;
    Node<T> right;

    Node(T data) {
        this.data = data;
        left = null;
        right = null;
    }
}

class CustomBinarySearchTree<T extends Comparable<T>> {
    private Node<T> root;

    public void insert(T item) {
        root = insertRec(root, item);
    }

    private Node<T> insertRec(Node<T> root, T item) {
        if (root == null) {
            root = new Node<>(item);
            return root;
```

```
        }
        if (item.compareTo(root.data) < 0) {
            root.left = insertRec(root.left, item);
        } else if (item.compareTo(root.data) > 0) {
            root.right = insertRec(root.right, item);
        }
        return root;
    }

    public boolean search(T item) {
        return searchRec(root, item);
    }

    private boolean searchRec(Node<T> root, T item) {
        if (root == null) {
            return false;
        }
        if (item.equals(root.data)) {
            return true;
        }
        if (item.compareTo(root.data) < 0) {
            return searchRec(root.left, item);
        }
        return searchRec(root.right, item);
    }
}

public class CustomBinarySearchTreeExample {
    public static void main(String[] args) {
        CustomBinarySearchTree<Integer> tree = new CustomBinarySearchTree<>();

        tree.insert(5);
        tree.insert(3);
        tree.insert(8);

        System.out.println("Contains 3? " + tree.search(3));
        System.out.println("Contains 6? " + tree.search(6));
    }
}
```

Output-

Contains 3? true
Contains 6? false

15. Write a Java Program that implements a custom circular queue data structure and performs enqueue and dequeue operations.

Code-

```
import java.util.ArrayList;
import java.util.List;

class CustomCircularQueue<T> {
  private List<T> queue = new ArrayList<>();
  private int front = -1;
  private int rear = -1;

  public void enqueue(T item) {
    if (isEmpty()) {
      front = rear = 0;
      queue.add(item);
    } else {
      rear = (rear + 1) % queue.size();
      if (rear == front) {
        queue.add(rear, item);
        front = (front + 1) % queue.size();
      } else {
        queue.set(rear, item);
  }
    }
  }

  public T dequeue() {
    if (isEmpty()) {
      throw new IllegalStateException("Queue is empty");
    }
    T item = queue.get(front);
    if (front == rear) {
      front = rear = -1;
    } else {
      front = (front + 1) % queue.size();
    }
    return item;
```

```
    }

    public boolean isEmpty() {
        return front == -1 && rear == -1;
    }
}

public class CustomCircularQueueExample {
    public static void main(String[] args) {
        CustomCircularQueue<String> queue = new CustomCircularQueue<>();

        queue.enqueue("A");
        queue.enqueue("B");
        queue.enqueue("C");

        while (!queue.isEmpty()) {
            System.out.println("Dequeued: " + queue.dequeue());
        }
    }
}
```

Output-

```
Dequeued: A
Dequeued: B
Dequeued: C
```

16. Write a Java Program that implements a custom trie (prefix tree) data structure to store and search for words.

Code-

```
class TrieNode {
    TrieNode[] children = new TrieNode[26];
    boolean isEndOfWord;

    TrieNode() {
        isEndOfWord = false;
        for (int i = 0; i < 26; i++) {
            children[i] = null;
        }
    }
}
```

```
class CustomTrie {
    private TrieNode root;

    CustomTrie() {
        root = new TrieNode();
    }

    public void insert(String word) {
        TrieNode current = root;
        for (int i = 0; i < word.length(); i++) {
            int index = word.charAt(i) - 'a';
            if (current.children[index] == null) {
                current.children[index] = new TrieNode();
            }
            current = current.children[index];
        }
        current.isEndOfWord = true;
    }

    public boolean search(String word) {
        TrieNode current = root;
        for (int i = 0; i < word.length(); i++) {
            int index = word.charAt(i) - 'a';
            if (current.children[index] == null) {
                return false;
            }
            current = current.children[index];
        }
return current.isEndOfWord;
    }
}

public class CustomTrieExample {
    public static void main(String[] args) {
        CustomTrie trie = new CustomTrie();

        trie.insert("apple");
        trie.insert("banana");

        System.out.println("Contains 'apple'? " + trie.search("apple"));
```

```
        System.out.println("Contains 'cherry'? " + trie.search("cherry"));
    }
}
```

Output-

Contains 'apple'? true
Contains 'cherry'? false

17. Write a Java Program that implements a custom Least Recently Used (LRU) cache data structure.

Code-

```
import java.util.LinkedHashMap;
import java.util.Map;

class CustomLRUCache<K, V> extends LinkedHashMap<K, V> {
    private final int capacity;

    CustomLRUCache(int capacity) {
        super(capacity, 0.75f, true);
        this.capacity = capacity;
    }

    @Override
    protected boolean removeEldestEntry(Map.Entry<K, V> eldest) {
        return size() > capacity;
    }
}

public class CustomLRUCacheExample {
    public static void main(String[] args) {
        CustomLRUCache<Integer, String> cache = new CustomLRUCache<>(3);

        cache.put(1, "One");
        cache.put(2, "Two");
        cache.put(3, "Three");

        System.out.println(cache);
        cache.get(2);
        System.out.println(cache);

        cache.put(4, "Four");
```

```
        System.out.println(cache);
    }
}
```

Output-

```
{1=One, 2=Two, 3=Three}
{1=One, 3=Three, 2=Two}
{3=Three, 2=Two, 4=Four}
```

Practise Questions

1. Implement a custom stack data structure that supports the push, pop, and peek operations. Write a Java Program to demonstrate these operations.
2. Create a custom queue data structure that can enqueue and dequeue elements. Write a Java Program to simulate a queue of customers waiting in line and serving them one by one.
3. Implement a custom singly-Linked List data structure with methods to add, remove, and display elements. Write a Java Program to demonstrate these operations.
4. Build a custom hash table data structure that supports key-value pairs and includes methods for inserting, retrieving, and removing elements. Write a Java Program to use this custom hash table.
5. Design a custom priority queue data structure that allows elements to be enqueued with a priority level and dequeued based on priority. Write a Java Program to demonstrate this custom priority queue.
6. Implement a custom circular doubly linked list data structure with methods for adding and removing elements in both forward and backward directions. Write a Java Program to demonstrate its functionality.
7. Create a custom red-black tree data structure that maintains its balance during insertion and deletion operations. Write a Java Program to demonstrate the functionality of this custom red-black tree.
8. Implement a custom tree (prefix tree) data structure to store and search for words efficiently. Write a Java Program to insert words into the tree and search for them.
9. Design a custom graph data structure with methods for adding vertices and edges. Write a Java Program to represent a simple graph and perform depth-first and breadth-first traversal.

**1.Write a program that compares the efficiency of two searching algorithms (e.g., linear search vs. binary search)
by measuring the time taken for each.**

Code-

```
import java.util.Arrays;

public class SearchComparisonExample {
    public static void main(String[] args) {
        int[] array = new int[1000000];
        Arrays.fill(array, 1);

        int target = 999999;

        long startTime = System.nanoTime();
        linearSearch(array, target);
        long endTime = System.nanoTime();
        long linearSearchTime = endTime - startTime;

        Arrays.sort(array);

        startTime = System.nanoTime();
        binarySearch(array, target);
        endTime = System.nanoTime();
        long binarySearchTime = endTime - startTime;

        System.out.println("Linear Search Time: " + linearSearchTime + " ns");
        System.out.println("Binary Search Time: " + binarySearchTime + " ns");
    }

    public static int linearSearch(int[] arr, int target) {
        for (int i = 0; i < arr.length; i++) {
            if (arr[i] == target) {
                return i;
            }
        }
        return -1;
    }
```

```
    public static int binarySearch(int[] arr, int target) {
        int left = 0;
        int right = arr.length - 1;

        while (left <= right) {
            int mid = left + (right - left) / 2;

            if (arr[mid] == target) {
                return mid;
            }

            if (arr[mid] < target) {
                left = mid + 1;
            } else {
             right = mid - 1;
            }
        }
        return -1;
    }
}
```

Output-

Linear Search Time: 5514129 ns

Binary Search Time: 8020 ns

2. Write a Java Program to count the number of elements in an array and analyze its time complexity using Big O notation.

Code-

```
public class CountArrayElements {
    public static void main(String[] args) {
        int[] array = {1, 2, 3, 4, 5, 6, 7, 8, 9, 10};
        int count = 0;

        for (int element : array) {
            count++;
        }

        System.out.println("Number of elements in the array: " + count);
    }
}
```

Output-
Number of elements in the array: 10
Time complexity- O(n)

3. Create a Java Program to compare Linear Search and Binary Search efficiency.
Code-

```
import java.util.Arrays;

public class SearchComparisonExample {
    public static void main(String[] args) {
        int[] array = new int[1000000];
        Arrays.fill(array, 1);

        int target = 999999;

        long startTime = System.nanoTime();
        linearSearch(array, target);
        long endTime = System.nanoTime();
        long linearSearchTime = endTime - startTime;

        Arrays.sort(array);

        startTime = System.nanoTime();
        binarySearch(array, target);
        endTime = System.nanoTime();
        long binarySearchTime = endTime - startTime;

        System.out.println("Linear Search Time: " + linearSearchTime + " ns");
        System.out.println("Binary Search Time: " + binarySearchTime + " ns");
    }

    public static int linearSearch(int[] arr, int target) {
        for (int i = 0; i < arr.length; i++) {
            if (arr[i] == target) {
                return i;
            }
        }
        return -1;
    }
```

```
    public static int binarySearch(int[] arr, int target) {
        int left = 0;
        int right = arr.length - 1;

        while (left <= right) {
            int mid = left + (right - left) / 2;

            if (arr[mid] == target) {
                return mid;
            }

            if (arr[mid] < target) {
                left = mid + 1;
            } else {
                right = mid - 1;
            }
        }
        return -1;
    }
}
```

Output-

Linear Search Time: 5514129 ns

Binary Search Time: 8020 ns

4. Write a Java Program for counting elements in an array and analysing time complexity.

Code-

```
public class CountArrayElements {
    public static void main(String[] args) {
        int[] array = {1, 2, 3, 4, 5, 6, 7, 8, 9, 10};
        int count = 0;

        for (int element : array) {
            count++;
        }

        System.out.println("Number of elements in the array: " + count);
    }
}
```

Output-

Number of elements in the array: 10

Time Complexity- O(n)

5. Write a Java Program to find the largest element in an array and analyze its time complexity using Big O notation.

Code-

```
public class FindLargestElement {
    public static void main(String[] args) {
        int[] array = {10, 45, 23, 67, 89, 54, 32, 78, 12, 98};
        int largest = findLargestElement(array);
        System.out.println("Largest element in the array: " + largest);
    }

    public static int findLargestElement(int[] arr) {
        int largest = arr[0];
        for (int i = 1; i < arr.length; i++) {
            if (arr[i] > largest) {
                largest = arr[i];
            }
        }
        return largest;
    }
}
```

Output-

Largest element in the array: 98

Time Complexity: O(n)

6. Implement a Java Program to perform a selection sort on an array and explain its time complexity using Big O notation.

Code-

```
public class SelectionSort {
    public static void main(String[] args) {
        int[] array = {64, 25, 12, 22, 11};
        selectionSort(array);
        System.out.println("Sorted array: " + Arrays.toString(array));
    }

    public static void selectionSort(int[] arr) {
        int n = arr.length;
        for (int i = 0; i < n - 1; i++) {
            int minIndex = i;
```

```
        for (int j = i + 1; j < n; j++) {
          if (arr[j] < arr[minIndex]) {
            minIndex = j;
          }
        }
        int temp = arr[minIndex];
        arr[minIndex] = arr[i];
        arr[i] = temp;
      }
    }
}
```

Output-

Sorted array: [11, 12, 22, 25, 64]

Time Complexity- O(n^2)

7. Implement a Java Program for a bubble sort algorithm and analyze its time complexity.

Code-

```
public class BubbleSort {
    public static void main(String[] args) {
        int[] array = {64, 34, 25, 12, 22, 11, 90};
        bubbleSort(array);
        System.out.println("Sorted array: " + Arrays.toString(array));
    }

    public static void bubbleSort(int[] arr) {
        int n = arr.length;
      for (int i = 0; i < n - 1; i++) {
        for (int j = 0; j < n - i - 1; j++) {
          if (arr[j] > arr[j + 1]) {
            int temp = arr[j];
            arr[j] = arr[j + 1];
            arr[j + 1] = temp;
          }
        }
      }
    }
}
```

Output-

Sorted array: [11, 12, 22, 25, 34, 64, 90]

Time Complexity- O(n^2)

Practise Questions

1. Write a Java Program to calculate the Fibonacci sequence up to a specified number and explain its time complexity.
2. Write a Java Program to perform a merge sort on an array, and explain its time complexity using Big O notation. How does merge sort compare to other sorting algorithms in terms of efficiency?
3. Compare and contrast the time complexities of linear search and binary search algorithms. Provide examples of scenarios where each algorithm is more efficient.
4. Write a Java Program that analyze the time complexity of a loop that iterates through an array of size "n" and performs a constant-time operation on each element.
5. Compare the efficiency of recursive and iterative algorithms. Provide examples where recursion might be less efficient and explain how the same problem can be solved iteratively.

1. Write a Java Program to find the factorial of the number.

Code-

```
class Fact
{
        public static void main(String[] args)
        {
                int number = 5;
                int factorial = number;
                for(int i =(number - 1); i > 1; i--)
                {
                        factorial = factorial * i;
                }
        System.out.println("Factorial of a number is:" + factorial);
        }
}
```

Output-

Factorial of a number is:120

2.Write a Java Program to display Fibonacci series.

Code-

```
import java.util.Scanner;
public class Fibonacci
{
        public static void main(String[] args)
        {
                int n, a = 0, b = 0, c = 1;
                Scanner s = new Scanner(System.in);
                System.out.print("Enter value of n:");
                n = s.nextInt();
                System.out.print("Fibonacci Series:");
                for(int i = 1; i <= n; i++)
                {
                        a = b;
                        b = c;
                        c = a + b;
                        System.out.print(a+" ");
                }
        }
```

```
}
```

Output-

Enter value of n: 5

Fibonacci Series: 01123

3. Write a Java Program to find whether the give number is Armstrong number or not.

Code-

```
import java.io.*;

class ArmStrong {
   public static void main(String[] args) throws IOException {
      int t, s = 0, n, r;
      System.out.println("Enter number:");
      BufferedReader br = new BufferedReader(new InputStreamReader(System.in));
      n = Integer.parseInt(br.readLine());
      t = n;
      while (t > 0) {
         r = t % 10;
         s = s + r * r * r;
         t = t / 10;
      }
      if (n == s)
         System.out.println("Number given is Armstrong");
      else
         System.out.println("Number given is not Armstrong");
   }
}
```

Output-

Enter number:153

Number given is Armstrong

4. Write a Java Program to reverse the given string.

Code-

```
import java.io.*;
import java.util.*;
class RevStr
{
    public static void main(String[] args) throws IOException
    {
                String or, rev="";
```

```
            DataInputStream dis=new DataInputStream(System.in);
            System.out.println("Enter String:");
            or=dis.readLine();
            int len=or.length();
            for(int i=len-1;i>=0;i--)
            {
            rev=rev+or.charAt(i);
            }
            System.out.println("Reverse of a string:"+rev);
        }
}
```

Output-

Enter String:siva
Reverse of a string:avis

5. Write a Java Program to evaluate quadratic equation

Code-

```
import java.io.*;
class QudEq
{
    public static void main(String args[])throws IOException
        {
            BufferedReader br;
            int a,b,c;
            double x,y,z;
            System.out.println("ENTER a VALUE:");
            br= new BufferedReader(new InputStreamReader(System.in));
            a=Integer.parseInt(br.readLine());
            System.out.println("ENTER b VALUE:");
            b=Integer.parseInt(br.readLine());
            System.out.println("ENTER c VALUE:");
            c=Integer.parseInt(br.readLine());
            z=Math.sqrt(b*b-4*a*c);
            x=(-b+Math.sqrt(b*b-4*a*c))/(2*a);
            y=(-b-Math.sqrt(b*b-4*a*c))/(2*a);
            if(z>0)
                {
                    System.out.println("THE REAL SOLUTIONS ARE ="+x+"\t"+"Y="+y);
            }
            else
```

```
            {
            System.out.println("THERE ARE NO REAL SOLUTIONS");
            }
    }
}
```

Output-

Enter a value:

4

Enter b value:

6

Enter c value:

-2

THE REAL SOLUTIONS ARE X=0.28077640640441515 Y==-1.780776406404415

6. Write a Java Program to count number of words in a given text.

Code-

```
import java.io.*;
import java.util.*;
class CountWords
{
    public static void main(String[] args) throws IOException
    {
            BufferedReader br=new BufferedReader(new InputStreamReader(System.in));
            System.out.println("Enter a string : ");
            String str=br.readLine();
            int count=0;
            if(str.length()==0)
            {
                    System.out.println("No.of words in given text:" + count);
            }
            else
            {
                    for(int i=0;i<str.length();i++)
                    {
                        if(str.charAt(i)==' ')
                    {
                            count++;
                    }
            }
```

```
            System.out.println("No.of words in given text:" + (count+1));
        }
    }
}
```

Output-

Enter a string:
hi this is siva
No.of words in given text:
4

7. Write a Java Program to check the given string is palindrome or not.

Code-

```
import java.io.*;
public class Palindrome
{
    public static void main(String args[]) throws IOException
    {
        BufferedReader br=new BufferedReader(new InputStreamReader(System.in));
        System.out.println("Enter String:");
         String str=br.readLine();
         char ch[]=new char[str.length()];
         for(int i=str.length()-1,j=0;i>=0;i--,j++){
                ch[j]=str.charAt(i);
                String restr=new String(ch);
                System.out.println("Reverse of String "+str+" is "+restr);
                }if(str.compareTo(restr)==0)
                        System.out.println(str+" "+"is a Palindrome");
                else
                         System.out.println(str+" "+"is not a Palindrome");
         }
}
```

Output-

Enter String:
madam
Reverse of String madam is madam
madam is a Palindrome

8. Write a Java Program to print the prime numbers upto nth number

Code -

```
import java.io.*;
class Primenos
{
	public static void main(String args[])throws IOException
	{
		BufferedReader br;
		int i,t,flag,n;
		br=new BufferedReader(new InputStreamReader(System.in));
		System.out.println("ENTER n VALUE:");
		n=Integer.parseInt(br.readLine());
		System.out.println("PRIME NUMBERS UP TO"+" "+n+":");
		for(i=2;i<=n;i++)
		{
			flag=1;
			for(t=2;t<i;t++)
			{
				if(i%t==0)
				{
					flag=0;
					break;
				}
			}
			if(flag==1)
			System.out.println(i);
		}
	}
}
```

Output-

```
ENTER n VALUE:
5
PRIME NUMBERS UP TO 5:
2
3
5
```

9. Write a Java Program to create a square pattern of asterisks.

Code-

```
public class SquarePattern {
```

```
    public static void main(String[] args) {
        int n = 4;
        for (int i = 0; i < n; i++) {
            for (int j = 0; j < n; j++) {
                System.out.print("* ");
            }
            System.out.println();
        }
    }
}
```

Output-

```
* * * *
* * * *
* * * *
* * * *
```

10. Write a Java Program to create an inverted right triangle pattern.

Code-

```
public class InvertedRightTrianglePattern {
    public static void main(String[] args) {
        int n = 4;
        for (int i = 0; i < n; i++) {
            for (int j = n; j > i; j--) {
                System.out.print("* ");
            }
            System.out.println();
        }
    }
}
```

Output-

```
* * * *
* * *
* *
*
```

11. Write a Java Program to create a pyramid pattern.

Code-

```
public class PyramidPattern {
    public static void main(String[] args) {
   int n = 4;
```

```
        for (int i = 0; i < n; i++) {
            for (int j = 0; j < n - i - 1; j++) {
                System.out.print(" ");
            }
            for (int k = 0; k <= i; k++) {
                System.out.print("* ");
            }
            System.out.println();
        }
    }
}
```

Output-

```
   *
  * *
 * * *
* * * *
```

12. Write a Java Program to create a diamond pattern.

Code-

```
public class DiamondPattern {
    public static void main(String[] args) {
        int n = 4;
        for (int i = 0; i < n; i++) {
            for (int j = 0; j < n - i - 1; j++) {
                System.out.print(" ");
            }
            for (int k = 0; k <= i; k++) {
                System.out.print("* ");
            }
            System.out.println();
        }
        for (int i = n - 2; i >= 0; i--) {
            for (int j = 0; j < n - i - 1; j++) {
                System.out.print(" ");
            }
            for (int k = 0; k <= i; k++) {
                System.out.print("* ");
            }
            System.out.println();
        }
```

```
    }
}
```

Output-

```
   *
  * *
 * * *
* * * *
 * * *
  * *
   *
```

13. Write a Java Program to create a number pyramid pattern.

Code-

```
public class NumberPyramidPattern {
    public static void main(String[] args) {
        int n = 4;
        for (int i = 1; i <= n; i++) {
            for (int j = 1; j <= n - i; j++) {
                System.out.print(" ");
            }
            for (int k = 1; k <= i; k++) {
                System.out.print(i + " ");
            }
            System.out.println();
        }
    }
}
```

Output-

```
   1
  2 2
 3 3 3
4 4 4 4
```

14. Write a Java Program to create a alphabetic pattern.

Code-

```
public class AlphabeticPattern {
    public static void main(String[] args) {
        int n = 4;
        char ch = 'A';
```

```
        for (int i = 1; i <= n; i++) {
            for (int j = 1; j <= i; j++) {
                System.out.print(ch + " ");
            }
            ch++;
            System.out.println();
        }
    }
}
```

Output-

```
A
B B
C C C
D D D D
```

15. Write a Java Program to create a half diamond pattern with numbers.

Code-

```
public class HalfDiamondNumberPattern {
    public static void main(String[] args) {
        int n = 5;
        for (int i = 1; i <= n; i++) {
            for (int j = 1; j <= i; j++) {
                System.out.print(j + " ");
            }
            System.out.println();
        }
        for (int i = n - 1; i >= 1; i--) {
            for (int j = 1; j <= i; j++) {
                System.out.print(j + " ");
            }
            System.out.println();
        }
    }
}
```

Output-

```
1
1 2
1 2 3
1 2 3 4
1 2 3 4 5
```

```
1 2 3 4
1 2 3
1 2
1
```

16. Write a Java Program to create a alphabetical pyramid pattern.

Code-

```
public class AlphabetPyramidPattern {
    public static void main(String[] args) {
        int n = 5;
        for (int i = 0; i < n; i++) {
            char ch = 'A';
            for (int j = 0; j < n - i - 1; j++) {
                System.out.print(" ");
            }
            for (int k = 0; k <= i; k++) {
                System.out.print(ch + " ");
                ch++;
            }
            System.out.println();
        }
    }
}
```

Output-

```
    A
   A B
  A B C
 A B C D
A B C D E
```

17. Write a Java Program to create a number triangle pattern.

Code-

```
public class NumberTrianglePattern {
    public static void main(String[] args) {
        int n = 4;
        int num = 1;
        for (int i = 0; i < n; i++) {
            for (int j = 0; j <= i; j++) {
                System.out.print(num + " ");
```

```
            num++;
        }
        System.out.println();
    }
  }
}
```

Output-

```
1
2 3
4 5 6
7 8 9 10
```

18. Write a Java Program for Method overloading.

Code-

```
public class Sum {

    // Overloaded sum(). This sum takes two int parameters
    public int sum(int x, int y) {
        return (x + y);
    }

    // Overloaded sum(). This sum takes three int parameters
    public int sum(int x, int y, int z) {
        return (x + y + z);
    }

    // Overloaded sum(). This sum takes two double parameters
    public double sum(double x, double y) {
        return (x + y);
    }

    // Driver code
    public static void main(String args[]) {
        Sum s = new Sum();
        System.out.println(s.sum(10, 20));
        System.out.println(s.sum(10, 20, 30));
        System.out.println(s.sum(10.5, 20.5));
    }
}
```

Output-

30

60

31.0

19. Write a Java Program to display the employee details using Scanner class.

Code-

```
import java.util.Scanner;

public class EmployeeDetails {
  public static void main(String[] args) {
    Scanner scanner = new Scanner(System.in);

    System.out.println("Enter Employee Details:");
    System.out.print("Employee Name: ");
    String name = scanner.nextLine();

    System.out.print("Employee ID: ");
    int employeeID = scanner.nextInt();

    System.out.print("Salary: ");
    double salary = scanner.nextDouble();

    System.out.println("\nEmployee Details:");
    System.out.println("Name: " + name);
    System.out.println("Employee ID: " + employeeID);
    System.out.println("Salary: " + salary);

    scanner.close();
  }
}
```

Output-

Enter Employee Details:

Employee Name: John Smith

Employee ID: 12345

Salary: 50000.0

Employee Details:

Name: John Smith

Employee ID: 12345

Salary: 50000.0

20. Write a Java Program to Implement a Stopwatch.

Code-

```
public class Stopwatch {
  public static void main(String[] args) throws InterruptedException {
    long startTime = System.currentTimeMillis();
    Thread.sleep(2000); // Sleep for 2 seconds
    long endTime = System.currentTimeMillis();
    long elapsedTime = endTime - startTime;
    System.out.println("Elapsed Time: " + (elapsedTime / 1000.0) + " seconds");
  }
}
```

Output-

Elapsed Time: 2.002 seconds

21. Write a Java Program to implement the Tower of Hanoi.

Code-

```
public class TowerOfHanoi {
  public static void main(String[] args) {
    int numDisks = 3;
    solveTowerOfHanoi(numDisks, 'A', 'B', 'C');
  }
  static void solveTowerOfHanoi(int n, char source, char auxiliary, char target) {
    if (n == 1) {
      System.out.println("Move disk 1 from " + source + " to " + target);
      return;
    }
    solveTowerOfHanoi(n - 1, source, target, auxiliary);
    System.out.println("Move disk " + n + " from " + source + " to " + target);
    solveTowerOfHanoi(n - 1, auxiliary, source, target);
  }
}
```

Output-

Move disk 1 from A to C
Move disk 2 from A to B
Move disk 1 from C to B
Move disk 3 from A to C
Move disk 1 from B to A
Move disk 2 from B to C
Move disk 1 from A to C

22. Program to Find the GCD (Greatest Common Divisor) of Two Numbers.

Code-

```
public class GCDCalculator {
    public static void main(String[] args) {
        int num1 = 48, num2 = 18;
        int gcd = findGCD(num1, num2);
        System.out.println("GCD of " + num1 + " and " + num2 + " is " + gcd);
    }

    static int findGCD(int a, int b) {
        if (b == 0) {
            return a;
        }
        return findGCD(b, a % b);
    }
}
```

Output-

GCD of 48 and 18 is 6

23. Program to Generate a Random Number between a Range.

Code-

```
import java.util.Random;

public class RandomNumberGenerator {
    public static void main(String[] args) {
        int min = 1;
        int max = 100;
        Random random = new Random();
        int randomNumber = random.nextInt(max - min + 1) + min;
        System.out.println("Random Number between " + min + " and " + max + ": " +
randomNumber);
    }
}
```

Output-

Random Number between 1 and 100: 22

24. Program to Convert Decimal to Binary.

Code-

```
public class DecimalToBinary {
```

```
    public static void main(String[] args) {
        int decimalNumber = 25;
        String binary = Integer.toBinaryString(decimalNumber);
        System.out.println("Binary representation of " + decimalNumber + " is " + binary);
    }
}
```

Output-

Binary representation of 25 is 11001

25. Write a Java Program to find the longest substring without repeating characters.

Code-

```
import java.util.HashMap;
import java.util.Map;

public class LongestSubstringWithoutRepeatingChars {
    public static void main(String[] args) {
        String str = "abcabcbb";
        int maxLength = findLongestSubstring(str);
        System.out.println("Longest Substring without Repeating Characters: " + maxLength);
    }

    static int findLongestSubstring(String s) {
        Map<Character, Integer> charIndexMap = new HashMap<>();
        int maxLength = 0;
        int startIndex = 0;

        for (int endIndex = 0; endIndex < s.length(); endIndex++) {
            char c = s.charAt(endIndex);
     if (charIndexMap.containsKey(c)) {
                startIndex = Math.max(startIndex, charIndexMap.get(c) + 1);
            }
            charIndexMap.put(c, endIndex);
            maxLength = Math.max(maxLength, endIndex - startIndex + 1);
        }

        return maxLength;
    }
}
```

Output-

Longest Substring without Repeating Characters: 3

26. Write a Java Program to implement Interface using extends keyword.

Code-

```
interface Inf1 {
   public void method1();
}

interface Inf2 extends Inf1 {
   public void method2();
}

public class Demo implements Inf2 {
   /* Even though this class is only implementing the interface Inf2, it has to implement all
   the methods of Inf1 as well because the interface Inf2 extends Inf1 */
   public void method1() {
      System.out.println("method1");
   }

   public void method2() {
      System.out.println("method2");
   }

   public static void main(String args[]) {
      Inf2 obj = new Demo();
      obj.method2();
   }
}
```

Output-

method2

27. Write a Java Program to represent Abstract class with example.

Code-

```
// Abstract class that contains an abstract method.
abstract class Shape {
   abstract void numberOfSides();
}

// Classes that illustrate the abstract method.
class Trapezoid {
   void numberOfSides() {
      System.out.println("The number of sides in trapezoidal are: 6");
```

```
    }
}

class Triangle {
    void numberOfSides() {
        System.out.println("The number of sides in triangle are: 3");
    }
}

class Hexagon {
    void numberOfSides() {
        System.out.println("The number of sides in hexagon are: 6");
    }
}

// Class that creates objects and calls the method.
class ShapeDemo {
    public static void main(String args[]) {
        Trapezoid obj1 = new Trapezoid();
        Triangle obj2 = new Triangle();
        Hexagon obj3 = new Hexagon();
        obj1.numberOfSides();
        obj2.numberOfSides();
        obj3.numberOfSides();
    }
}
```

Output-

The no. of sides in trapezoidal are: 6
The no. of sides in triangle are: 3
The no. of sides in hexagon are: 6

28. Write a Java Program to implement solution of producer consumer problem.

Code-

```
import java.util.LinkedList;

public class ThreadExample {
    public static void main(String[] args) throws InterruptedException {
        // Object of a class that has both produce() and consume() methods
        final PC pc = new PC();
```

```
    // Create producer thread
    Thread t1 = new Thread(new Runnable() {
      @Override
public void run() {
        try {
          pc.produce();
        } catch (InterruptedException e) {
          e.printStackTrace();
        }
      }
    });

    // Create consumer thread
    Thread t2 = new Thread(new Runnable() {
      @Override
      public void run() {
        try {
          pc.consume();
        } catch (InterruptedException e) {
          e.printStackTrace();
     }
      }
    });

    // Start both threads
    t1.start();
    t2.start();

    // t1 finishes before t2
    t1.join();
    t2.join();
  }

  // This class has a list, producer (adds items to the list), and consumer (removes items).
  public static class PC {
    // Create a list shared by producer and consumer
    // Size of the list is 2.
    LinkedList<Integer> list = new LinkedList<>();
    int capacity = 2;
```

```
    // Function called by the producer thread
    public void produce() throws InterruptedException {
        int value = 0;
        while (true) {
  synchronized (this) {
                // Producer thread waits while the list is full
                while (list.size() == capacity)
                    wait();
                System.out.println("Producer produced-" + value);
          // To insert the jobs in the list
                list.add(value++);
                // Notifies the consumer thread that
                // now it can start consuming
                notify();
                // Makes the working of the program easier
                // to understand
                Thread.sleep(1000);
            }
        }
    }

    // Function called by the consumer thread
    public void consume() throws InterruptedException {
        while (true) {
            synchronized (this) {
                // Consumer thread waits while the list
                // is empty
                while (list.size() == 0)
                    wait();
                // To retrieve the first job in the list
                int val = list.removeFirst();
                System.out.println("Consumer consumed-" + val);
                // Wake up the producer thread
                notify();
                // and sleep
                Thread.sleep(1000);
            }
        }
    }
}
```

}

Output-

```
Producer produced-0
Producer produced-1
Consumer consumed-0
Producer produced-2
Consumer consumed-1
Producer produced-3
Consumer consumed-2
Producer produced-4
Consumer consumed-3
Producer produced-5
Consumer consumed-4
```

Additional Resources

YouTube Video Links-

Introduction of Java-https://youtu.be/D2ixfO5_Jac

OOP's Concept-https://youtu.be/psb5GhfbIMk

Introduction To Microsoft SQL Server- https://youtu.be/ea8J7PsfaEc

DBMS Introduction- https://youtu.be/SwB6RTAQ-o0

Introduction of MySQL -https://youtu.be/-7NOhrJoDko

Best Java Frameworks for Web Development in2024 -https://youtu.be/ulXx-OJFgME

Online Resources

Core Java Programming Online Test Paper Link- https://forms.office.com/r/gzYwDiE3JQ
Scan QR Code for Online Test Paper-

YouTube Video Link – https://youtu.be/QBGPXiFvD6U
Scan QR Code for YouTube Video -

In this book

In this comprehensive book, you will embark on a journey into the fundamentals of Java, exploring its core concepts, syntax, and application in real-world scenarios. Whether you're a beginner looking to build a strong foundation or an experienced developer seeking to master Java's intricacies, this book will equip you with the knowledge and skills needed to become a proficient Java Programmer. Dive into the world of Object-Oriented Programming, Data Structures, Multi-threading, and unleash the power of Java to develop robust and scalable applications."